The Power to Lead

The Power to Lead

A Guidebook for School Administrators on Facilitating Change

Frank Siccone
Siccone Institute, San Francisco

Allyn and Bacon
Boston · London · Toronto · Sydney · Tokyo · Singapore

ISBN 0-205-14345-8

Printed in the United States of America

10 9 8 7 6 5 4 3   01 00 99 98

Dedication

To my brother, Robert Siccone, for his many contributions to me and my family. Growing up, he was my big brother and constant companion. Now, he and his family — children and grandchildren — continue to add meaning to my life and provide me with moments of profound joy.

The choices you made, Bob, afforded me the freedom to explore, realize and fulfill myself and my purpose. Thank you.

The book is also dedicated to Mary and Edward Vecchia — my other parents — for instilling in me the values of self-determination, appreciation of family and pride of achievement.

Contents

PART II *Leadership of Others:*
Facilitating Relationships   **70**

Introduction   71

3   Communicating   72

4   Coaching   101

Introduction

"The educational foundations of our society are presently being eroded by a rising tide of mediocrity that threatens our very future as a nation and a people."

With this alarmist call for change, the modern school reform movement was born in 1983 with the publication of the report, **A Nation at Risk: The Imperative for School Reform** released by the National Commission of Excellence in Education.

Eight years later, with the realization that a significant infusion of attention, energy and money — spending per pupil was increased by 29 percent in "real" dollars — yielded virtually no results, the need for change was echoed, once again, with the introduction of **America 2000: An Education Strategy**. In announcing the program, then President Bush said, "For the sake of the future of our children and our nation, we must transform America's schools. The days of the status quo are over."

In spite of these high-level proclamations, and many similar reports issued during subsequent years, actual improvement seems elusive. Test scores remain essentially flat. More than a quarter of high school students fail to graduate with the classmates with whom they started. Only five percent of students graduating from American high schools can read at a level that would qualify them for entry into a European university. At the start of 1995, the number of state university students in California lacking basic math and English skills had grown so high — approaching half of all freshmen at some campuses — that university officials are considering dramatic new approaches to the problem such as establishing an institute on school reform to work within the kindergarten to 12th grade system to help make improvements.

Another study conducted in 1995 — the first national survey ever done by the Census Bureau of hiring, training and management practices in U.S. business — revealed that employers lack confidence in the ability of schools and colleges to prepare young people for the workplace. They claim that one-fifth of U.S. workers are not fully proficient in their jobs. In fact, American companies are spending an estimated $20 billion a year on remedial education programs. Illustrating an alarming division between the schools and the workplace, the study, produced for the federal Department of Education, found that employers tended to disregard grades and school evaluations in selecting workers.

Schools, of course, serve a broader educational purpose than just training workers, but if students are not being prepared for either work or for higher education, what do we envision their futures will be like, and what role does education have in helping secure these?

It seems that rather than measurable improvement, what has been happening during the past dozen or more years has been debates over missions and methodologies:

- Should school reform efforts be initiated on a national level involving politicians, business people and other professionals, or should it be left to teachers, administrators and parents at the local level?

- Should parents be given a choice as to which schools to send their children, or would this decimate public education and further divide wealthy families from the poor and middle class?

- Should schools be measured on the basis of how well they prepare youth for the workplace?

- Are national standardized test scores a true assessment of student competence? As Dr. Ulysses Van Spiva, president of the Council of Urban Boards of Education, suggests, "Testing kids does not make them smarter any more than weighing pigs make them heavier."

- Is offering remedial classes to make up for the failure of the K-12 system the responsibility of universities, or should they be reserved for higher levels of academic training?

• Is "reforming," "restructuring," or "re-engineering" the best approach to improving schools?

The real problem seems to be that American public schools are being asked to do a job they were never designed to do. As Edward Fiske, former education editor of The New York Times says, "Trying to get more learning out of the current system is like trying to get the Pony Express to compete with the telegraph by breeding faster ponies."

Public schools, which are essentially nineteenth century institutions organized around an industrial model, are being asked to educate people for life in the twenty-first century. A whole new approach — one appropriate to the Information Age and to our being a "thinking society" — is needed. More of the same — more basic skills classes, more time spent in schools, even more money — won't help if the basic structure is not radically transformed.

To turn out students who can think, schools must be thinking organizations. Transforming school will not work as a top-down, externally-mandated, one-size-fits-all program. The people who will be affected by the changes must be thoughtful participants in the process.

Leadership is an essential ingredient for success, but a particular type of leadership is required. "Leader as facilitator" is the style that empowers others to be creative thinkers and active contributors.

Schools can not be transformed except through the transformation of the individuals who make up the school community. So, in a sense, transformative leadership exists in four domains: within yourself; your relationships with colleagues; teams or subgroups within the school; and the school as an entire organization.

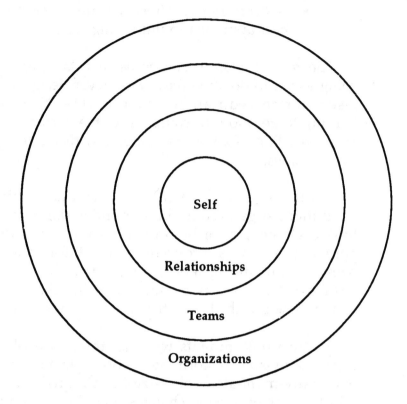

Self

Relationships

Teams

Organizations

Domains of Leadership

The Power to Lead provides you with an extensive sequence of activities to enable you to facilitate change at all four of these Domains of Leadership.

Part One — the first phase of the process — is intended to support you in being a visionary leader with a clear and focused mission. Next, Part Two focuses on building collaborative relationships with staff by emphasizing effective communication skills and coaching strategies. Facilitating teams — running effective meetings, shared decision making and collaborative problem solving — follows in Part Three. Finally, Part Four addresses transformation at the organizational level with exercises in strategic planning and managing the change process.

You may wish to use this book by following the structure of the four stages and implementing the activities as sequenced. It would also work for you to select sections of the text that are most relevant to the needs of your school at this time, and to use these activities to facilitate change where it will make the biggest difference.

Now, more than ever, your courage and commitment are needed to help schools deliver on their promise of creating a better world through the development of an enlightened citizenry.

It may often seem hopeless as we are all being asked to do more with less. Schools are more crowded. Resources are less available. Teachers are more frustrated. Parents are less involved. Students are more challenging and less prepared. Yet, none of us can give up: the stakes are too high. Every child deserves an opportunity to learn, to grow, to fulfill his or her full potential. We can not, we must not, fail them.

It is my sincere desire that this book serves in some small way to rekindle hope in you and your colleagues, and that it provides you with concrete action steps for achieving the dream that we all share.

Thank you for caring.

...The test of the extent and quality of power and leadership is the degree of actual accomplishment of the promised change.
—James MacGregor Burns

Acknowledgments

I am grateful to all of my clients — individuals as well as organizations — who provided opportunities for me to test this material on their real-world problems.

A very special thanks to Steve Darland for his consistent support of my work over the years. Consulting with him and the employees of J. Walter Thompson/West has been extremely rewarding for me.

Let me also express appreciation to some key educators with whom I've been privileged to work:
- Michele Burchfiel and the Union School District
- Joe Fimiani and the team at Santa Clara County Office of Education
- Bill Schmidt and all the staff at Lone Pine School District
- June Thompson and the extraordinary youth leaders with the California Association of Student Councils
- John Tweten and the San Jose Unified School District
- Holly Mannix and Dianne Maxon for personally taking the time to read the manuscript and provide helpful feedback, as well as for making it possible for me to work with the exceptional teachers at Marin Country Day School
- Lulu Lopez at the CSAP Violence Leadership Support Project and my fellow Board Member of the National Association for Self-Esteem, who also provided valuable editorial comments.

To other recent business clients:
- Ric Ensor and the teams at American President Lines
- Lou Hoffman and the staff at his agency
- Joan and Bob McGrath, Dennis Kakures and the great people at McGrath RentCorp

The philosophy and methodology reflected in this book have been influenced by many others in the fields of education and management consulting. Among those who were gracious enough to grant permission to have their work adapted for inclusion here, let me specifically mention George M. Gazda, Alec Mackenzie, The Community Board Program and Interaction Associates.

I also wish to acknowledge my dear colleagues Esther Wright, Hanoch McCarty and Jack Canfield for their continued friendship and encouragement. Thank you Robert Wright for the excellent job you did in preparing the manuscript. And to Chris Jehle for proofreading and editing, as well as saving my place on the beach.

Part I

Leadership of Self:
Facilitating Personal Effectiveness

> *I change myself, I change the world.*
> —Gloria Anzaldua

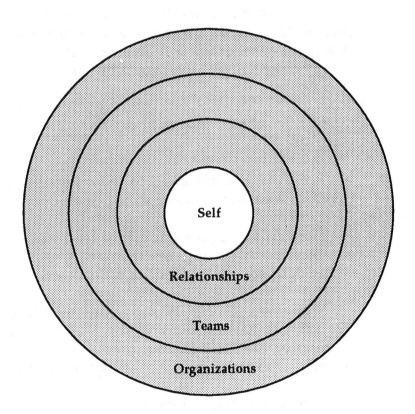

1

Part One   **Leadership of Self:**
Facilitating Personal Effectiveness

*Theories and goals of education don't matter a bit
if you don't consider your students to be human beings.*
—Lou Ann Walker

Introduction

What is your personal philosophy of education? What do you believe schools are designed to do?

Do schools exist so that society can inculcate students with a particular set of values? Is there a distinct body of knowledge that all students must learn in order to be considered culturally literate?

Is education a matter of economics: are there skills that businesses need their workers to have that schools are supposed to teach? To what extent is mandatory attendance in school primarily a way of keeping young people out of the workforce or at least off the streets?

Should schools be about preserving the past or preparing us for the future?

Are children blank slates to be written upon, lumps of clay to be molded, wild animals to be tamed or unique spirits to be nurtured?

How do you define the role of teachers: subject matter experts, facilitators of learning, disciplinarians, pseudo-parents, part-time counselors, educational leaders or followers of state mandates?

Who owns schools? Who is accountable to whom and for what? Do schools have "clients?" Are students and their parents the clients, or are students the product of schools, or are students workers who are being managed by teachers to produce knowledge?

In what business are you?

The activities in the first part of this chapter help you formulate your philosophy of education. This is a good place to begin because — examined or unexamined — your philosophy determines how you think about education, how you approach your job, what you value, how you feel and how you act.

To be a truly effective leader you must know where you are going, and to know where you are going you must know where you are coming from.

Chapter 1

From Vision to Action

I *have long since come to believe that people never mean half of what they say, and that it is best to disregard their talk and judge only their actions.*

—Dorothy Day

1 Purpose Does as Purpose Is

Nothing contributes so much to tranquilize the mind as a steady purpose — a point on which the soul may fix its intellectual eye.
—Mary Shelly

Purpose

As educators, most of us find a great deal of meaning in our work provided we stay connected with our true reason for being in education. By staying focused on what is really important to you, you will be better able to deal with the day-to-day challenges of the job.

This activity invites you to explore your most profound purpose, the significant value you contribute, what makes your work meaningful.

Procedure

1. Imagine yourself as having reached the age of the chronologically gifted (previously known as old age). You are retired and have been enjoying these golden years. From this perspective, reflect back on your life, the contributions you've made, the lives you've touched, and consider your legacy. How would you like to be remembered?

2. Now imagine receiving a letter from one of your former colleagues — perhaps a teacher in your school — or a student. Maybe there is one person in particular from whom you would like to hear, one of the many teachers or students who have been in your school.

3. Actually write a letter to yourself as if it came from this person. What would you want him or her to say? How would you want to be remembered? What lasting impact would you want to have had on this person's life?

4. After you have written the letter, read it over and see what it says about your real purpose for being in education.

5. Now use that letter as the basis from which to write a purpose statement — a one-sentence declaration of what you are

seeking to accomplish, what you most want to contribute to your staff and students.

2 Mission Control

He who has a why to live for can bear almost any how.
—Friedrich Nietzsche

Purpose

The **purpose** statement you wrote for the previous activity is a way of stating your reason for being. Your purpose came into existence when you did.

Your **mission** is a cause toward which you are working. For example, my purpose is to make a positive difference in the world and my mission is to contribute to creating schools where all students feel appreciated and competent.

Define your mission by following these four steps.

Procedure

1. What do you have/want to contribute? This might include your unique personal qualities or strengths, such as intelligence, creativity or leadership skills.

   _____

   _____

2. To whom or in what way do you want to contribute? This might include action words such as educate students or inspire teachers.

   _____

   _____

3. To what end? What will be the benefits of your contribution? Think in terms of positive outcomes such as empowered students, collaborative teams, or peaceful and productive schools.

   _____

   _____

   _____

4. Combine the three prior answers into a single statement.[*]

   Example: My mission is to use my commitment to young people and my leadership skills to collaborate with teachers and inspire students to work together in making our school a place where everyone experiences success.

   _____

   _____

   _____

[*] Adapted with permission from Jack Canfield (co-author, *Chicken Soup for the Soul*). This activity originally appeared in *101 Ways to Develop Student Self-Esteem and Responsibility* by Jack Canfield and Frank Siccone (Boston: Allyn and Bacon, 1993)

3 The Vision Thing

Any of us can dream, but seeking vision is always done not only to heal and fulfill one's own potential, but also to learn to use that potential to serve all our relations: the two-leggeds, the four-leggeds, the wingeds, those that crawl upon the Earth, and the Mother Earth herself.

—Brooke Medicine Eagle

Purpose

In 1960, President John F. Kennedy declared our country's commitment to "put a man on the moon by the end of the decade." This served as a very powerful *strategic vision* that directed the people who worked on the space program. Education needs a similar vision — something to strive for that is so obviously great that it inspires passion and evokes committed action.

Procedure

1. Given the mission statement that you just wrote in the last activity, ask yourself the following question:

   - What is the greatest achievement I could imagine accomplishing in my school in the next five years?

2. Other questions to explore:

   - If someone I consider to be a great teacher or leader (such as Confucius, Socrates, Black Elk, John Dewey, Helen Keller, Maria Montessori, Marva Collins, and so on) were asked the same question, what would he or she define as the greatest possible achievement?
   - If I had a student in my school on whom the future of the world depended, what type of educational environment would I provide for this child? What does my choice of environment say about my vision for all students?
   - If I were to win the Nobel Peace Prize for my work in education, what would they cite as my major achievements?
   - What educational objectives could I be working toward that would really motivate me to be enthusiastic about school every day?

- What do I think is really needed at my school (even if I have discarded this idea in the past as being too idealistic)?
- From the teachers' perspective, what is most needed?
- From the students' perspective, what is most needed?
- From the parents' perspective, what is most needed?
- From the business community's perspective, what is most needed?
- From society's perspective, what is most needed?

3. Using your answers to these questions, write a one-sentence statement of your **strategic vision.**

4. Once you have defined your vision, share it with at least one colleague. Sharing your vision with others will make it more real to you. It will also feel more possible after you share it.

The most successful leader of all is one who sees another picture not yet actualized. He sees the things which belong in his present picture but which are not yet there.... Above all, he should make his co-workers see that it is not his purpose which is to be achieved, but a common purpose, born of the desires and the activities of the group.

—Mary Parker Follett

4 Value Pack

*W*hat is a cynic? A man who knows the price of everything and the value of nothing. And a sentimentalist...is a man who sees an absurd value in everything, and doesn't know the market price of any single thing.

—Oscar Wilde

Purpose

The staff at one of my client school districts identified over thirty different educational objectives that they felt were important. This activity is based upon the recognition that there is only so much time you and your staff have on any given day, only so much you can focus on at any given time and only so many resources you have available.

If your school could only do a few things — and do them well — which ones would you choose?

Procedure

1. You'll need a stack of index cards or Post-it® Notes, sized to fit within the boxes drawn on the Value Pack Worksheet (2"x2-1/2").

2. Writing one idea on each index card or Post-it® Note, identify as many educational objectives and school-related priorities as possible. (A sample list is included for your reference.)

3. Now, pick the top six objectives you feel are most important in an effective school, and place the cards in order on the worksheet; the objective in space one being the most important, and so forth.

   When you have finished placing all six cards in the appropriate spaces, consider what this reveals about what you most value.

4. If you were doing this process from the viewpoint of being a parent, which six objectives would you choose to have be the focus of your child's school? Are they the same ones you

11

picked before or do you want different things for your own child than you want for other children?

If you knew your child had the potential of being a great world leader, what six educational objectives would you value?

Would your top six values change if you knew your child only had one year to live?

5. Consider which values changed, if any, with the different scenarios and which remained constant. What does this say about what really matters to you? How adequately is your school environment currently meeting these educational objectives? What more could you be doing to provide leadership in this area?

6. You may want to have your staff do this exercise to audit the school's values as part of a Strategic Planning Process (see Chapter 9, Activities 65 - 76).

POSSIBLE EDUCATIONAL OBJECTIVES
AND SCHOOL-RELATED PRIORITIES

- Learning basic skills
- Learning thinking skills
- Learning study skills
- Learning computer skills
- Developing creative talents
- Learning communication skills
- Learning problem-solving skills
- Appreciating diversity and multicultural awareness
- Learning about good health and physical education
- Enhancing self-esteem, and personal and social responsibility
- Learning interpersonal-relationship and parenting skills
- Becoming life-long learners
- Developing leadership skills
- Providing a safe and secure environment
- Having high expectations of students
- Accounting for developmental stages of children and young adults
- Accommodating students' learning styles and rates of learning
- Providing a balanced education
- Using an integrated approach that shows the relationship of all subjects
- Using a Whole Language approach
- Using a team-teaching approach
- Using authentic assessment instruments such as portfolios
- Using computers and other technology as an integral part of the learning process
- Using cooperative learning methods
- Providing an effective counseling program
- Increasing parent involvement
- Developing a strong partnership between the school and community

VALUE PACK WORKSHEET

(1)	(2)
(3)	(4)
(5)	(6)

5 A Day in the Life

In great matters men show themselves as they wish to be seen; in small matters as they are.

—Gamaliel Bradford

Purpose

In the previous activity, you decided on six educational objectives that you consider most important to an effective school. Let's look at how these relate to your job functions.

How can you as a school administrator use your position, energy and time to help your school achieve these educational objectives? How does this compare with how you actually spend your time and energy?

Procedure

1. Using the Worksheet, Ideal Day, divide the daily schedule into sections representing how you think you really should be spending your work time.

   Possible categories might include:
   — coaching staff on instructional methods
   — facilitating staff/community school improvement teams
   — increasing parent involvement
   — building school/business partnerships
   — fundraising
   — attending district-level meetings
   — managing school finances
   — overseeing facilities maintenance
   — handling student discipline problems

   See if you can take the six most important educational objectives and translate these into your job specifications.

2. Next, using the Worksheet, Current Day, section off what portion of your day you actually spend on any of these various aspects of your job.

3. Note the discrepancy between the real and the ideal and set goals for yourself to move in the direction of being able to do what is most important to you.

IDEAL DAY WORKSHEET

Time	
7:00 AM	_____
7:30	_____
8:00	_____
8:30	_____
9:00	_____
9:30	_____
10:00	_____
10:30	_____
11:00	_____
11:30	_____
12:00 PM	_____
12:30	_____
1:00	_____
1:30	_____
2:00	_____
2:30	_____
3:00	_____
3:30	_____
4:00	_____
4:30	_____
5:00	_____
5:30	_____
6:00	_____

CURRENT DAY WORKSHEET

7:00 AM	_____
7:30	_____
8:00	_____
8:30	_____
9:00	_____
9:30	_____
10:00	_____
10:30	_____
11:00	_____
11:30	_____
12:00 PM	_____
12:30	_____
1:00	_____
1:30	_____
2:00	_____
2:30	_____
3:00	_____
3:30	_____
4:00	_____
4:30	_____
5:00	_____
5:30	_____
6:00	_____

6 Be SMART about Setting Goals

*W*ithout some goal and some efforts to reach it,
no man can live.

—Fyodor Dostoevsky

Purpose

The first few activities in this section provided opportunities to do some goal setting. The purpose of this activity is to suggest guidelines for refining your goals so that they are more likely to be achieved.

Procedure

1. Select one of the goals that you identified in one of the previous activities. Using the SMART Goals Worksheet, apply each of the five guidelines to your goal.

   - Specific

        Most people state their goals in very general terms — to make more money, to lose weight, to be happy and healthy.

        The more specific you can be and the more detail you use in describing your goal, the greater the likelihood of achieving it — how much more money? How much less weight? What could you achieve that would make you happy? What could you do to improve your health?

   - Measurable

        Describing your goal in measurable terms is a way of being more specific. Some goals are easily quantifiable — How much? How many? To what degree? By what percentage?

        Goals that cannot be quantified can be made measurable by asking yourself the questions: How will I know that I've achieved it? To what will I look for evidence?

- Achievable

   Is your goal realistic? Do you have a past track record that would indicate that what you want to accomplish in the future is possible?

   Considering how you will go about achieving the goal, through what means, will often help to reveal whether it is do-able.

- Responsible

   Responsibility has two dimensions — response/ability
   responsiveness or willingness
   and
   ability or control.

   Is this goal one that you are willing to achieve? Is it something that you truly desire or did you set this goal because you thought you should. (As someone once said, "Don't should on yourself.")

   Secondly, do you have the ability to achieve this goal? Is it within your control? If someone else actually controls the outcome of this goal, do you at least have some influence? How can you rewrite your goal so that it reflects the part over which you do have control?

- Timeframe

   Establishing a deadline by when something will be completed is an excellent way of reinforcing your commitment to the goal. Once the end date is set, you can work backwards to determine the timeframe for all the interim steps leading to the final goal.

SMART GOALS — WORKSHEET

Are you being S M A R T about your goals?

S pecific — What specifically do you intend to achieve?

_____

_____

_____

M easurable — How will you know when you've achieved it?

_____

_____

_____

A chievable — Is it realistic?

_____

_____

_____

R esponsible — Are you willing to be responsible for it. Is it **desirable**? Are you **able** to be responsible for it? Is it **controllable**?

_____

_____

_____

T imeframe — By when will you have accomplished it?

_____

_____

_____

7 Mastering Life

It has begun to occur to me that life is a stage I'm going through.

—Ellen Goodman

Purpose

On the road to achieving one's goals, "stuff happens." People who are successful accept what happens as part of the process — learn from it, gain insights, make appropriate corrections — and proceed toward their goals. People who are not successful treat what happens as insurmountable obstacles or as evidence that they are not able to achieve their goals, and then they drop out.

The current dropout rate among today's students suggests that many of them desperately need to learn how to deal more effectively with the challenges of achieving success. The purpose of this activity is to support you in mapping out the path to success, and in accepting whatever happens as part of the process.

Procedure

1. Get a large piece of paper and some colored markers.

2. Start by placing an X somewhere on the page to represent *where you are now* (like the "You Are Here" signs found in parking garages and shopping malls).

3. Next draw a picture of your goal on the page, an appropriate distance from "where you are now." Use signs, symbols, or words to represent the goal you identified in the previous activity.

4. Now draw in the *milestones* to be accomplished as you progress from where you are now to the completion of your goal. Each milestone represents an objective that will be achieved as part of this process.

5. Next consider possible *obstacles*, roadblocks, or barriers that could get in the way of your accomplishing your goal, and draw these on your page.

6. Finally, put in the *resources* available to you to overcome these obstacles. These can include both internal resources (such as patience, self-confidence, and determination) as well as external resources (such as colleagues, friends, classes, and books).

7. You could also do this exercise with your staff.

8 The First Step

*To achieve your goal, a vision of the peak is needed,
For the first step depends upon the last.
But do not mistake the vision for the reality,
For the last step depends upon the first.*

—Old Chinese Saying

Purpose

Now it is time to take action. With your goal identified, you are ready to define some action steps.

Procedure

1. Using the "First Step Worksheet," consider the first objective to be achieved between where you are now and your goal.

2. Using this objective as a focal point, set a date by when it is to be accomplished.

3. Working chronologically backward from this objective, write down all the individual action steps that need to be taken during this period of time.

4. Now determine what one thing you can complete in the next 24 hours toward achieving your objective. Integrate this into whatever system you use to organize your schedule (such as a calendar or daily planner).

5. How will you measure your success? How will you know when you have completed the task?

6. Now, make a commitment to yourself to complete these steps accepting whatever happens as part of the process.

*People who say it cannot be done
should not interrupt those who are doing it.*

—Anonymous

FIRST STEP — WORKSHEET

1. First major objective

   _____

   _____

2. Date by when this goal is to be achieved _____

3. *Action Step*   *Completion Date*

   _____   _____

   _____   _____

   _____   _____

   _____   _____

   _____   _____

   _____   _____

4. Immediate next step (within 24 hours)

   _____

   _____

5. Measurement of success

   _____

   _____

Chapter 2

Timing is Everything

The time is always right to do what is right.
—Martin Luther King, Jr.

9 Buying Time

We work not only to produce but to give value to time.
—Eugene Delacroix

Purpose

The last chapter helped you recognize the degree to which you are spending your time in areas that are likely to make the biggest difference.

This organization and time management assessment instrument will help you discover ways you can save time and redirect your energies.

Procedure

1. Complete the Organization and Time Management Assessment Instrument by circling the number next to each item which best describes the frequency with which you engage in these behaviors.

2. Review your responses. Acknowledge yourself for those items where you *Usually* (3) or *Almost always* (4) act wisely.

   Study the areas that are rated *Almost never* (0) or *Sometimes* (1) for these offer the opportunity for greatest improvement. Use this information to direct yourself to the section in this chapter that relates to your improvement areas.

ORGANIZATION AND
TIME MANAGEMENT — WORKSHEET

ASSESSMENT INSTRUMENT

	Almost never 0	Sometimes 1	Half the time 2	Usually 3	Almost always 4

SETTING GOALS AND PRIORITIES					
1. I know the goals, objectives and priorities of my organization (district, school, teaching team)......	0	1	2	3	4
2. Priorities are communicated and agreed upon within my school......	0	1	2	3	4
3. I translate these goals into monthly, weekly and daily goals for myself......	0	1	2	3	4
4. My goals are SMART and I measure my progress frequently......	0	1	2	3	4

PLANNING THE WORKDAY					
5. I spend time every day planning the best use of my time......	0	1	2	3	4
6. I set realistic time estimates on tasks......	0	1	2	3	4
7. I build cushions into my day to allow for unforeseen crises......	0	1	2	3	4
8. I maintain a Master List — a single place where all action items are recorded......	0	1	2	3	4
9. I use an appointment book or calendar to record all scheduled activities......	0	1	2	3	4

HANDLING PAPERWORK					
10. I keep my work space organized so that tasks can be accomplished in order of priority and distractions are minimized...	0	1	2	3	4
11. I manage paperwork efficiently and have a system that allows me to handle each piece of paper only once......	0	1	2	3	4
12. Up-to-date filing systems are maintained to optimize speed of retrieval......	0	1	2	3	4

ASSESSMENT INSTRUMENT - Continued

Almost never 0	Sometimes 1	Half the time 2	Usually 3	Almost always 4

DELEGATING EFFECTIVELY

13. I seek opportunities to delegate whenever possible.. 0   1   2   3   4

14. When I delegate a project, I communicate clearly the purpose, intended result, timeline, and performance standards........ 0   1   2   3   4

15. I ask for feedback on the effectiveness with which my delegation style empowers the staff person......................... 0   1   2   3   4

MANAGING THE DELEGATORS

16. When a project is delegated to me, I take the time to be sure that I understand the job specifications...................................... 0   1   2   3   4

MANAGING PROJECTS

17. When I manage a project, I set up a system that monitors WHAT needs to be done, BY WHOM and BY WHEN............................ 0   1   2   3   4

MASTERING TIME WASTERS

18. I refer to my priority goals when interrupted or unexpected items occur in order to decide the best use of my time...... 0   1   2   3   4

19. I have strategies in place to avoid being interrupted by phone calls and drop-in visitors (e.g. screening calls, voice mail, setting time limits, referring the caller or visitor to someone else, etc.)...................... 0   1   2   3   4

20. I am able to say no to low-value or otherwise inappropriate requests............. 0   1   2   3   4

ASSESSMENT INSTRUMENT - Continued

Almost never 0	Sometimes 1	Half the time 2	Usually 3	Almost always 4

MASTERING TIME WASTERS- Continued

21. I only call meetings when necessary and use a number of tactics to make sure that they are productive (e.g. right people attend, material sent out beforehand, agenda with time limits, start and end on time, etc.)... 0   1   2   3   4

22. I only attend meetings that are relevant and actively seek ways to help make them more productive.............................. 0   1   2   3   4

23. When I notice that I am procrastinating, I employ a tactic to get myself going........... 0   1   2   3   4

24. When I travel on business, I am organized to make productive use of my time........... 0   1   2   3   4

10 Who Knows Where the Time Goes*

I've been on a calendar, but never on time.

—Marilyn Monroe

Purpose

This activity will give you factual data on how you spend your time so that you can be more effective in controlling it to better advantage.

Procedure

1. Make ten copies of the Time Log Worksheet.

2. For the next two weeks, keep a daily record of how you spend your time. You can do this by recording what you are doing at fifteen minute intervals throughout the day or by recording the time you begin each new activity.

   At the start of each day list your three major goals for the day at the top of the worksheet indicating their ranking — 1,2 or 3 — and the amount of time you estimate each will take.

3. At the end of the day check to see if you achieved your three major goals. Also note how you actually spent your time, how much time was spent on various types of activities. In the column labeled Value, record a 1 if the activity was both important and urgent, a 2 if it was important but not urgent, 3 if it was urgent but not important, 4 if you feel the activity was a waste of time, and 5 if it was a routine activity such as commuting.

   In the last column, indicate whether you spent your time on activities you had planned or dealing with unexpected occurrences.

4. After maintaining your Time Log for two weeks, study where you can become more effective.

---

* This activity was adapted with permission from Alec MacKenzie, author of *The Time Trap* (New York: American Management Association, 1990)

- How often did you get all of your number 1 items done (Important and Urgent)?

- How often did you complete your goals for the day?

- How can you reduce the time you waste on unimportant items?

- How frequently did urgent (but not necessarily important) items take precedence?

- How can you minimize crises in the future?

- How can you make better use of your time when you are involved in routine tasks?

- How much of your time was spent dealing with the unexpected? How can you allow time for this when planning your workday in the future?

TIME LOG

Date _____

Priorities for Today

Rank	Goal	Time Estimated
_____	_____	_____
_____	_____	_____
_____	_____	_____

Actual Time Recording

Time	Activity	Time Used	Value *	P/U **

* 1. Important and Urgent (Must)   4. Wasted   ** Planned
  2. Important (Should)   5. Routine   Unexpected
  3. Urgent (Reacted)

11 Time Wasters

If it weren't for the last minute, nothing would get done.

—Anonymous

Purpose

The purpose of this activity is to help eliminate time wasters so that you have more time to spend on what really matters.

Procedure

1. Review your Time Logs (Activity 10) for those areas where you noted having wasted time. A list of typical time wasters is included for your reference.

2. Use the Time Wasters Worksheet to list the activities that most frequently waste your time.

3. Refer to the chart, Spheres of Influence, and record on your worksheet whether each Time Waster is a:
   1 — you are able to control
   2 — you are able to influence
   3 — unable to control or influence

4. For each Time Waster that you are able to control (1), identify a possible solution for eliminating it. The list of Time Savers may be helpful as you look for solutions.

   If the Time Waster is one that you can at least influence if not actually control (2), consider who is in control of this and how you could best get them to support you in not wasting time.

   If any of the Time Wasters are totally out of your control and influence (3), decide whether it is best to accept this as a given or to develop a plan whereby you could gain some influence in this area.

5. Begin immediately to act on the solutions you have identified.

TYPICAL TIME WASTERS

- Excessive interruptions

- Procrastination

- Non-productive conversations (i.e. gossiping, complaining, etc.)

- Playing "telephone tag"

- Not getting or giving clear instructions at the outset

- Trying to find something in a stack of papers or in a disorganized filing system

- Unnecessary or unproductive meetings

- Unnecessary memos

TIME SAVERS

- Determine priorities

- Distinguish between **important** (high payoff) tasks and **urgent** trivialities

- Know the purpose

- Delegate, whenever possible

- At the beginning of each day, plan — in detail — the work you intend to accomplish. List the tasks according to priority with the estimated amount of time needed

- Schedule time for important tasks

- At the end of the day, review your list to determine how much you accomplished

- Attend only the meetings or parts of meetings that involve you directly

- Use an agenda at meetings

- Schedule time to return phone calls early in the day or toward the end of the day

- Record due dates for assignments on your calendar

- When accepting assignments, write it down and read it back to check for accuracy

SPHERES OF INFLUENCE

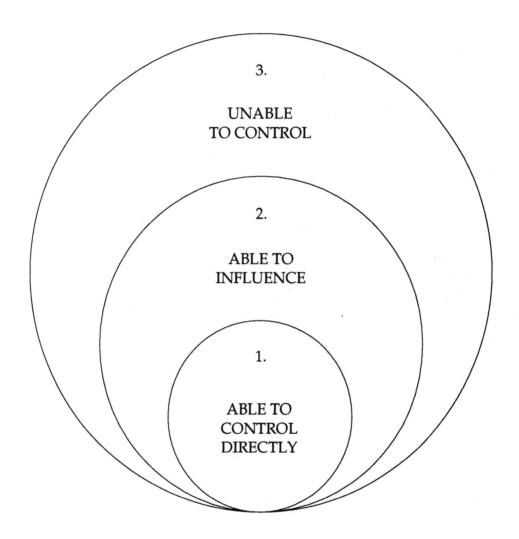

TIME WASTERS WORKSHEET

TIME WASTERS	SPHERE OF INFLUENCE	POSSIBLE SOLUTIONS

12 Planning Your Workday

There is nothing so useless as doing efficiently that which should not be done at all.

—Peter Drucker

Purpose

Today is the only part of your life that is available to you — everything else is either a memory of the past or a wish for the future.

In order to make the most of today, this activity gives you ideas for how to plan the best use of your time.

Procedure

1. Make a copy of the Daily Plan Worksheet.

    • Check your calendar for items that are due to be done today. If they are scheduled activities, record them on the right side of the Daily Plan. If they are unscheduled activities put them on the Things To Do Today list on the left hand side of the Daily Plan.

    • Review your Master List for action items that need to be completed today. The Master List is a single notebook that includes all Goals, Projects, Staff or Parent Requests, District Directives, Tasks, Errands, and so forth.

    • Prepare a list of the action items you can reasonably expect to complete today on the Things To Do Today side of the page.

    • Determine the value of each item:
        1. Important and Urgent
        2. Important
        3. Urgent
        4. Unimportant
        5. Routine

    • Establish the two most important priorities and estimate how long each will take to complete.

- Consider your schedule for the day (the right side of the page) and make an appointment with yourself to work on your top two priorities. Whenever possible, schedule your priority items during your "Prime Time,"* first thing in the morning or at your first available unscheduled period.

- After you have completed your top two priorities for the day, refer to your list of action items for the next most important task to be done.

- Allow time in your daily plan to deal with unexpected items.

- As other items arise throughout the day, assess whether they are more important that what you have already planned. If not, put the new tasks on your Master List to be dealt with later.

- At the end of the day, review what you actually accomplished relative to your action plan. Cross off the items that got completed in your Master List. Decide what to do about the items that did not get done today.
  — Do them tonight.
  — Put them on the list for tomorrow.
  — Leave them on the Master List for now.
  — Delegate them to someone else.
  — Admit that they are not important enough to do and drop them from your list. Communicate to anyone who might be affected by this decision.

---

* Prime Time is the time of day when you are able to work at peak performance, when you have the most energy and your concentration is sharpest.

DAILY PLAN WORKSHEET

Day _____ Date _____

THINGS TO DO TODAY

Priority	Est. Time	Value	
			_____
			_____
			_____
			_____
			_____
			_____
			_____
			_____
			_____
			_____
			_____

1 Important and Urgent
2 Important
3 Urgent
4 Unimportant
5 Routine

SCHEDULE

8:00	_____
8:30	_____
9:00	_____
9:30	_____
10:00	_____
10:30	_____
11:00	_____
11:30	_____
12:00	_____
12:30	_____
1:00	_____
1:30	_____
2:00	_____
2:30	_____
3:00	_____
3:30	_____
4:00	_____
4:30	_____
5:00	_____

DAILY PLAN WORKSHEET

Sample

Day _____ Date _____

SCHEDULE

8:00	Staff Meeting
8:30	Morning bell
9:00	
9:30	
10:00	Parent conference
10:30	Recess — yard duty
11:00	
11:30	Lunch — yard duty
12:00	
12:30	
1:00	Superintendent's Council
1:30	
2:00	
2:30	
3:00	→
3:30	SIP Meeting
4:00	→
4:30	
5:00	

THINGS TO DO TODAY

Priority		Est. Time	Value
2	Observe Classroom 5	30 min.	2
1	Prepare budget figures for Superintendent Meeting	30 min.	1
3	Call parents re: tardies	15 min.	5
4	Delegate making room arrangements for SIP Meeting		4

1 Important and Urgent
2 Important
3 Urgent
4 Unimportant
5 Routine

42

13 Most Important Reminders

Purpose

Virtually everyone feels they need more time; that there is always more to do than there are hours in the day.

The truth is that you already have all the time there is; the twenty-four hours available in a day. So, the issue is not making more time or managing your time better, it is really a matter of managing what you do with your time more effectively.

The purpose of this activity is to help you stay focused on what your real priorities are so that you take maximum advantage of the time you have.

Procedure

1. Take a piece of 8-1/2" x 11" paper (card stock is best) and fold it in thirds to make a tent card.

2. On each panel print one of these three questions:
   - "What is the best use of my time right now?"
   - "If I could only complete one task today, which one is most vital?"
   - "What do my 'clients' think is most important for me to do today?"

3. Place the tent card on your desk where you can see it easily and rotate the panels each day so that you will be constantly reminded to do what is most important.

14 Handling Paperwork — FAST!

The volume of paper expands to fill the available briefcase.
—Jerry Brown

Purpose

Many of us get bogged down in paperwork. Even with rapid advances in technology, the amount of paper coming across the desks of most administrators remains awesome. The paperless office seems a remote dream.

The purpose of this exercise is to help you sort through your paperwork FAST!

Procedure

All paperwork can pretty much be divided into four categories:

1. Information that you can delegate to someone else. Whenever possible — FORWARD IT.

2. Material that you must do yourself — ACT ON IT.

3. Items that do not require action by you or someone else but need to be filed for future reference — SAVE IT.

4. All pieces of paper that do not require action, for which there is no reason to keep or where copies are available elsewhere can be discarded — TOSS IT.

If you are fortunate enough to have a secretary who screens your paperwork for you, then ask him or her to use this system and only pass on to you the items you personally need to act on.

Otherwise, set aside a certain amount of time each day to go through your paperwork (approximately thirty minutes). Pick a time that works for you — probably not your "Prime Time" or times when more important priorities could be accomplished.

Do your best to handle each piece of paper only once. Remember F.A.S.T.

Forward It

If someone else is responsible for or interested in this area, pass it on. Delegate it to someone else, whenever possible. You can write a note on the actual document or attach a Post-it® with instructions for the other person. Put the item in your "OUT" box to be forwarded.

Act on It

Create a file folder labeled "ACTION ITEMS." If the item is one for which you are responsible, put it into your "action" folder. Refer to these when you plan your workday so that you can integrate them into your schedule and priorities system.

Save It

Make a file folder marked "TO FILE." If the item does not require action and you have a purpose for saving it, put it in your "to file" folder. Integrate these into your filing system on a regular basis (every couple of weeks depending upon the volume).

Toss It

Keep a recycling bin or wastebasket handy. If you have no purpose for holding onto this piece of paper or if duplicates are available, then discard it.

15 Managing Projects

A good manager is best when people barely know that he exists. Not so good when people obey and acclaim him. Worse when they despise him. Fail to honor people, they fail to honor you. But of a good manager, who talks little; when his work is done, his aim fulfilled, they will say, "We did this ourselves."

—Lao-tzu

Purpose

In addition to the routine tasks that make up the job of any school administrator, you are probably called upon to manage special projects whether it be a student activities program, staff in-service training schedule or district-level curriculum revision committee.

These guidelines will help you make a large, potentially overwhelming, project more manageable.

Procedure

Step 1   Determine the purpose and intended results; the purpose being what good the project is meant to serve and the result being the actual outcome. For example, the purpose of the Staff Development Program is to expand the ability of our teachers to help all students achieve.

The intended results include:
- teachers are better able to identify the learning styles of their students
- teachers acquire a set of strategies that are reflected in how they interact with students around learning.

Step 2   Establish the completion date. This end date will determine the overall timeframe for the project and its components.

Step 3   Break the project into sub-tasks. Depending upon the complexity of the project, you may need to identify sub-tasks for each of the major components of the project.

Step 4   Arrange the sub-tasks into a logical sequence. One way of doing this is to put each of the sub-tasks on index cards and then moving them around until an appropriate order has been determined.

Step 5   Develop a timeline by setting a due date for each sub-task.

Step 6   Assign sub-tasks. Decide on who will be responsible for completing the tasks.

Step 7   Monitor progress. Set up a project sheet: a list of WHAT tasks need to be done, BY WHOM and BY WHEN. Project sheets can be put in a section of your Master List, in a folder for the appropriate project or in your "Action" folder. Wall calendars can also be used to track project due dates. Complex projects may require more sophisticated methods such as a PERT/CPM (Program Evaluation and Review Technique/Critical Path Method) system. Project Management computer software is also available.

16 Delegating Effectively

Next to doing a good job yourself, the greatest joy is in having someone else do a first-class job under your direction.
—William Feather

Purpose

Depending on the size of your educational institution, its organizational structure and your position in it, your ability to delegate tasks to someone else may be limited. Funding cutbacks in many districts have reduced staff to such a degree that delegation is nearly impossible. In addition, union contracts often prohibit administrative work being passed on to teachers.

In some situations, it would be smart for the administrative team to re-evaluate its priorities and division of responsibilities. One of my client school districts — when faced with trying to meet ever-increasing demands with ever-diminishing resources, decided to bring some sanity back into their work lives.

The district office staff first defined who their "clients" were — students, parents and community, teachers and site administrators, the superintendent and school board. Next, they assessed what district output was most important to each group of clients.

Accepting these as their team goals, they then reassigned the tasks involved so that the workload was more evenly divided among each of the individual team members. Work that was not important to their clients was eliminated. Client expectations regarding what was possible for the district office staff to deliver were re-negotiated.

Some projects were taken on by site administrators and staff in collaboration with a district director.

If you are in a situation that allows you to delegate tasks to others, these guidelines help make it an opportunity for both of you.

Procedure

1. Make a list of activities for which you are currently responsible. Consider which tasks you must continue to perform yourself, which ones can be shared with staff and which ones can be delegated.

2. Analyze the tasks that can be shared and those that can be delegated in terms of the skills required to complete them successfully. Match the tasks with the skill set of each of your staff members to capitalize on their strengths. Also look for opportunities to assign tasks that will challenge people to develop new skills, especially in areas essential to their career advancement.

3. Assess the individual needs and abilities of each person and use a delegation style that will be effective for them. Ask them for feedback.

4. Create a clear, mutual understanding of the purpose of the assignment and the desired result. Focus on the **what**, rather than on the **how**; the **results** rather than the **methods**, so that the person doing the task feels a greater sense of ownership for it.

5. Establish the parameters within which the individual should operate. These guidelines should support the person in learning from the past experience of others without being overly confining.

6. Identify available resources — human, technical, financial and organizational.

7. Determine performance standards and specific times for reporting and evaluation.

8. Establish the degree of authority you are willing to delegate:

   — proceed without approval
   — proceed and keep me informed
   — proceed only after approval.

9. Maintain an appropriate degree of communication throughout the project to empower the employee, build trust, monitor progress, and ensure success.

10. When questions or problems arise, avoid giving answers or solutions. Ask the person what he/she thinks ought to be done. Use other questioning techniques to help them arrive at their own answers.

11. Avoid taking back the project if it runs into trouble. Support the person in completing it or, if necessary, delegate it to someone else.

12. Be sure the person who did the work gets the credit.

17 Overcoming Procrastination

Someday is not a day of the week.

—Anonymous

Purpose

Whether due to fear of failure — or fear of success — people often sabotage themselves. Putting things off until the last minute and then doing a less than exemplary job is an all too common form of self-sabotage.

Since procrastination is really a symptom, it can be helpful to diagnose the underlying cause.

In some instances the source of the problem is that the project is unpleasant, boring or meaningless, or seems too difficult and overwhelming.

In other cases — especially when procrastination has become a consistent pattern of behavior — the cause is more deeply rooted. Afterall, one of the benefits of throwing something together at the last minute is the comforting illusion that had you taken more time you could have done an excellent job. An acceptable excuse that cushions you from the fear that just maybe your best work might not really be good enough.

Here are some guidelines to help you breakout of procrastination paralysis.

1. If the project seems too difficult or overwhelming, chunk it down into smaller tasks and begin with these.

2. If the project is boring, consider delegating it to someone for whom it would be an exciting challenge.

3. If the project seems meaningless, define the purpose for doing it. If you see no purpose for it, find out what the purpose is of the person who initiated the project. If no one has a purpose for it, question whether it really needs to be done. If you are required to do it anyway, create your own purpose; one that would make it worth your time and effort.

4. If the project is unpleasant, consider starting with the more interesting parts first and then letting the momentum get you through the rest. You might enlist the support of a partner to help with the project, or make it a team effort, or delegate it or parts of it.

5. Make firm time commitments to yourself, the client, your manager and/or the team that will support your working on the project.

6. Commit to working on the project for at least a short period of time (i.e. thirty minutes). It won't be so hard to start and you may discover that it is not all that bad once you get started.

7. Schedule an appointment with yourself to work on the project, and treat this as seriously as you would any appointment.

8. Plan ways to reward yourself after you have completed the project as well as at key points along the way.

18 Keeping Your Life in Balance

There is more to life than increasing its speed.
—Mohandas Gandhi

Purpose

This activity is an invitation to explore how your work as an educator fits into the larger context of your life as a whole.

Most would agree that the purpose of schools is to help youngsters become well-rounded human beings. This exercise will support you in being a model of someone who successfully balances personal and professional goals.

Procedure

1. Get a pencil, a copy of the five-page Strategic Plan for Your Life Worksheet, and a watch or time piece.

2. Using the timer, give yourself two minutes to write down your lifetime goals. These are things you want to accomplish sometime during your life. They may be related to your job, career, or profession; to your family and friends; to money, lifestyle, and personal possessions; to important things you want to achieve; or to ways you want to enjoy yourself.

3. At the end of two minutes, stop writing. Now, take another two minutes to read over what you wrote, make any changes you want, and put your lifetime goals in order of priority. (1 = most important, 2 = next most important, and so on.)

4. When time is up, complete this part of the activity by writing down the purpose of the goal that was the highest on your list of priorities. Give yourself one minute to complete your purpose statement. Examples:

   Goal 1:   To provide for my family.

   Purpose: To share love and closeness, and to raise children who will grow up to make a contribution to the world.

Goal 1: To become superintendent of a large school district.

Purpose: To have greater influence over how schools are run so that I can help students become effective adults.

5. Next, turn to the second page of the worksheet.

   Write your five-year goals. These are the things you want to accomplish in the next five years. Consider the same categories as you did with the lifetime goals. Take two minutes to make your list.

   When time is up, take two more minutes to review what you wrote, make changes, and put your five-year goals in order of priority.

   Finish this part of the activity by writing a purpose statement for your number 1 goal.

6. Next, turn to the third page of your worksheet. Repeat the process for your six-month goals. Consider the same categories. Again, take two minutes to make your list.

   Then, spend two more minutes revising and ranking your list of six-month goals.

   Finally, write the purpose of your number 1 six-month goal.

7. Now turn to the next page of the worksheet. Write your one-month goals. Take two minutes to come up with your list.

   Then take two more minutes to review and rank your list.

   To complete the one-month goals, write a statement of purpose for your number 1 goal.

8. Now, review the goals you wrote on these four worksheets and consider the following questions:

   How were your one-month goals different from your lifetime goals?

   What did you discover about your number 1 goal as you moved from long-term to short-term goals?

What is the connection between your number 1 lifetime goal and your number 1 one-month goal?

Is your number 1 short-term goal the next step on the path toward achieving your lifetime goal? If not, consider whether there is another short-term goal that is really number 1, or whether there is a different lifetime goal that is more important to you than the one you identified as number 1.

9. Now, what if you found out that you only had a month to live? What would be important to you? How would your goals change? How would you spend the next 30 days if you knew that these were the last 30 days of your life?

Use the fifth page of the worksheet to list your goals for your last month following the same procedure as the others in terms of timing and so forth.

Complete this activity by reflecting on what implications it has for how you live your life on a day-to-day basis.

STRATEGIC PLAN FOR MY LIFE — WORKSHEET

LIFETIME GOALS

What goals would you like to accomplish during your lifetime? Consider all areas of your life such as: career, home/family/relationships, physical/emotional/spiritual well-being, community involvement/public service, travel/leisure/hobbies, and so forth.

GOAL   PRIORITY

_____   _____
_____   _____
_____   _____
_____   _____
_____   _____
_____   _____
_____   _____
_____   _____
_____   _____
_____   _____
_____   _____

PURPOSE OF PRIORITY GOAL

_____
_____
_____
_____
_____
_____
_____
_____

STRATEGIC PLAN FOR MY LIFE — WORKSHEET
(Continued)

FIVE YEAR GOALS

Given your lifetime ambitions, what do you want to have accomplished within the next five years? Focus on the goals areas that are most relevant to this time in your life.

GOAL   PRIORITY

_____   _____

_____   _____

_____   _____

_____   _____

_____   _____

_____   _____

_____   _____

_____   _____

_____   _____

_____   _____

PURPOSE OF PRIORITY GOAL

_____

_____

_____

_____

_____

_____

_____

STRATEGIC PLAN FOR MY LIFE — WORKSHEET

SIX MONTH GOALS

What are some short-term actions you can take toward advancing your five-year goals?
What can you realistically accomplish during the next six months?

GOAL   PRIORITY

_____   _____

_____   _____

_____   _____

_____   _____

_____   _____

_____   _____

_____   _____

_____   _____

_____   _____

_____   _____

_____   _____

PURPOSE OF PRIORITY GOAL

_____

_____

_____

_____

_____

_____

_____

STRATEGIC PLAN FOR MY LIFE — WORKSHEET

ONE MONTH GOALS

What can you do immediately relative to your goals? What can you accomplish over the next three or four weeks?

GOAL   PRIORITY

_____   _____

_____   _____

_____   _____

_____   _____

_____   _____

_____   _____

_____   _____

_____   _____

_____   _____

_____   _____

_____   _____

PURPOSE OF PRIORITY GOAL

_____

_____

_____

_____

_____

_____

_____

STRATEGIC PLAN FOR MY LIFE — WORKSHEET

LAST MONTH GOALS

When time is of the essence, what really matters to you?

GOAL   PRIORITY

_____   _____

_____   _____

_____   _____

_____   _____

_____   _____

_____   _____

_____   _____

_____   _____

_____   _____

_____   _____

_____   _____

_____   _____

PURPOSE OF PRIORITY GOAL

_____

_____

_____

_____

_____

_____

_____

60

19 Pie in the Sky

How we spend our days is, of course, how we spend our lives.
—Annie Dillard

Purpose

Building upon the previous activity, this exercise is designed to have you recognize the gap between how you are currently spending your time and what would be a more ideal situation for you.

Procedure

1. Using the worksheet, My Life Currently, divide the pie chart into sections representing the portion of time you currently spend on certain activities.

    The following categories may be used:
    • work/career
    • recreation/hobbies
    • relationships/family
    • sleep/routine
    • community service/spiritual growth

2. Now, using the worksheet, My Life in Balance, divide the pie chart into segments that represent the amount of time you would ideally like to spend in each of the activity categories.

3. Compare the two charts and note the discrepancy between the ideal and the real.

4. Select the area or areas that are most important for you to change, and set a goal or goals for yourself to move in the direction of a more balanced life.

MY LIFE CURRENTLY — WORKSHEET

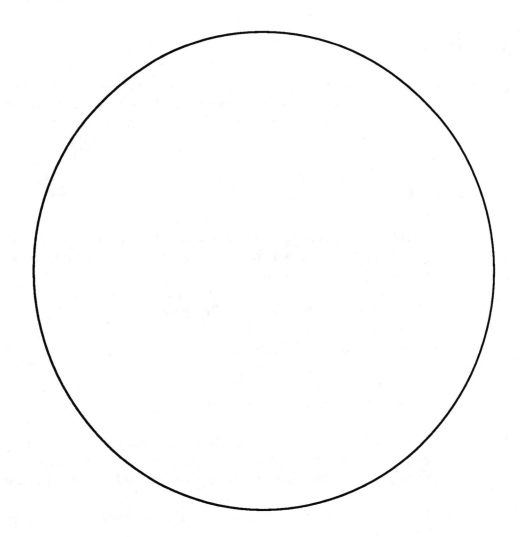

MY LIFE IN BALANCE — WORKSHEET

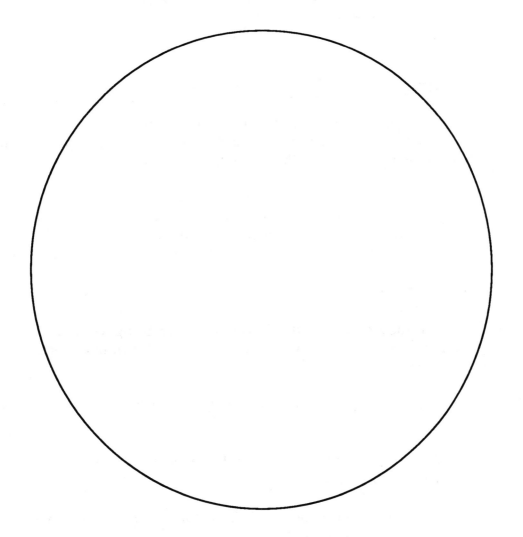

20 Avoiding Transition Traps

Life is easier than you'd think; all that is necessary is to accept the impossible, do without the indispensable, and bear the intolerable.

— Kathleen Norris

Purpose

In the process of making changes in one's life — even positive ones — people often sabotage themselves or encounter problems with others who are used to the status quo.

The purpose of this activity is to support you in moving beyond your old habits by considering potential traps that you might stumble upon during the transition.

Procedure

Before moving forward on your plans to bring your life more in balance, reflect upon these questions and the implications of your answers.

- In order to get your life in balance, what would you need to do more frequently?

- In order to get your life in balance, what would you need to do less frequently?

- What will you most enjoy about the changes? What will be the benefits to you and others?

- In making the changes necessary to bring your life in balance, what will you miss most?

- What concerns or fears do you have about making these changes?

- Who else would be affected by these changes and how are they likely to react?

- Whose permission do you need in order to achieve a more balanced life?

- Will the tasks that you are looking to reduce or eliminate for yourself still need to be done? If so, who else could do them?

- What other support and resources will you need?

- What is the timeframe for the transition?

- What are your immediate next steps?

- How committed are you to getting your life in balance?

21 Goals Follow-Up

*I don't want to get to the end of my life
and find that I lived just the length of it.
I want to have lived the width of it as well.*

—Diane Ackerman

Purpose

Just in case you think that the goals you set for yourself earlier in this chapter have been forgotten, here is a follow-up exercise to help keep you on track.

Procedure

Select one of the important goals you set for yourself and use the appropriate worksheet depending upon whether you were successful in achieving your goal or not.

GOAL ACCOMPLISHED WORKSHEET

What was the goal you set for yourself?

_____

_____

What specifically did you do?

_____

_____

To what do you attribute your success?

_____

_____

How do you feel about your accomplishment?

_____

_____

What worked for you in support of your success?

_____

_____

What did you learn from this?

_____

_____

Were there any points along the way that were difficult and/or where things didn't work?

_____

_____

What did you learn from this?

_____

_____

Would you say this goal was too easy? Too difficult? Challenging yet realistic enough of a stretch to be a real accomplishment?

_____

Based upon your experience of this, what is your goal for the next period of time?

_____

_____

GOAL NOT ACCOMPLISHED WORKSHEET

What was the goal you set for yourself?

_____

_____

What happened?

_____

_____

How do you feel about what happened?

_____

_____

In what way was this what you expected?

_____

_____

What happened that was unexpected?

_____

_____

What didn't work?

_____

_____

What did you learn from this?

_____

_____

Were there points along the way when you were successful?

_____

_____

What worked?

_____

_____

What did you learn from this?

_____

_____

GOAL NOT ACCOMPLISHED WORKSHEET
(Continued)

What are the consequences of your not having achieved your goal?

_____

_____

On a scale of 1-10, how committed would you say you were?

_____

Is this goal still important to you?

_____

What is your purpose in accomplishing this?

_____

_____

Based upon your experience this time, how will you modify your goal?

_____

_____

What will you do differently in achieving the goal?

_____

_____

What other resources or support do you feel you need?

_____

_____

On a scale of 1-10, how committed would you say you are to accomplishing this goal?

_____

Part II

Leadership of Others:
Facilitating Relationships

> **W**e find ourselves not independently of other people and institutions but through them. We never get to the bottom of our selves on our own. We discover who we are face to face and side by side with others in work, love and learning.
>
>   —Robert N. Bellah, et al.

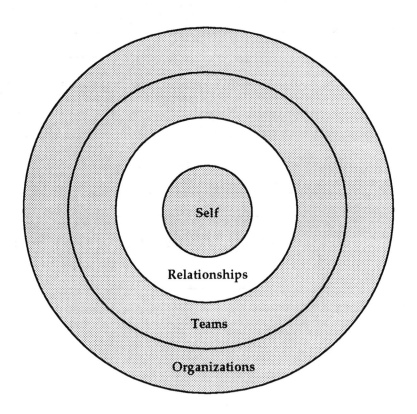

Part Two   Leadership of Others: Facilitating Relationships

*B*reath is life, and the intermingling of breaths is the purpose of good living. This is in essence the great principle on which all productive living must rest, for relationships among all the beings of the universe must be fulfilled; in this way each individual life may also be fulfilled.

—Paula Gunn Allen

Introduction

Relationships are the building blocks of organizations. Your success in facilitating change at your school will depend, for the most part, on how well you relate to people one-on-one.

This part focuses on two of your roles as an educational leader: communicator and coach.

Education is communication. Knowledge is transferred through communication. Skills are gained through communication. Even character building and moral development depends on communication. Without communication, learning cannot occur.

Coaching is a term used to describe a style of managing designed to encourage people to contribute their best. Coaching recognizes that employees are not just another pair of hands to be used to get more work done, but rather that they are full human beings with heads and hearts and souls. When people — especially teachers, to whom we entrust our children and youth — are treated with this type of respect, everyone gains.

Whereas supervisors control, coaches empower.

Chapter 3

Communicating

Self-expression must pass into communication for its fulfillment.

—Pearl Buck

22 What is Communication?

In the right key, one can say anything. In the wrong key, nothing. The only delicate part is the establishment of the key.
— George Bernard Shaw

Purpose

If you think about it — actually analyze how you spend your time — you will probably notice that it all boils down to communication. On a moment by moment basis, your job, for the most part, consists of someone delivering and/or receiving a communication.

Obviously, the more effective you are as a communicator, the more successful you will be at work — in fact, in all areas of your life.

So, what exactly is communication? How does communication happen?

The purpose of this activity is to deepen your understanding of communication. Activities that follow will give you tools to increase your effectiveness as a communicator.

Procedure

1. On a piece of paper using a pencil or colored markers draw a diagram or schematic of how you think communication occurs. Find graphic ways — signs, symbols, figures, and so forth — to illustrate how people communicate. Do this first before proceeding to the next step.

2. When you have completed your drawing of the communication process, read the following list of questions and reflect on any insights you gain that you might want to include in your drawing.

   • Since communication — as with similar words such as community, communion and so forth — means to share or have in common, the word suggests that communication involves at least two people.

Does your diagram of communication depict two communicators?

- Communication links two or more parties: a connection is established.

  Does you image show a connection?

- Communication is most effective when it is a two-way exchange, not just one person talking at another.

  Is the idea of two-way communication depicted in your drawing?

- Communication occurs verbally and non-verbally, and it involves the exchange of meaning, not just words.

  Is there a way that you've captured this idea in your diagram?

3. As a way of facilitating communication among your colleagues, select the people with whom you work most closely and invite them to do this exercise.

   Meet with them one-on-one or in a group to share diagrams and discuss the communication process.

23 Not by Words Alone
The Three Dimensions of
Communication

Education is learning what you didn't even know you didn't know.

—Ralph Waldo Emerson

After a presentation I gave to some 300 or so parents, I was touched by one of the mothers who came up to me after the talk to thank me for my comments. She said she gained a lot of value from my ideas and went on to say that it was clear to her that I "had a personal relationship with the Lord." There was no reference to religion in my presentation, yet from her viewpoint my remarks were consistent with her beliefs.

Later that evening when I was reading some written evaluations of my presentation, I was struck by the comment "Dr. Siccone and his humanistic philosophy shouldn't be allowed in our schools." Being familiar with the school of thought linking self-esteem with the New Age Movement, I understood that some people view humanism as atheism, since it is a philosophy that locates the human being as the source of power in one's life — a position reserved by many religions as God's rightful role. That two people in the same audience heard two completely opposite messages was particularly intriguing.

How is this possible?

Obviously, there is more to communication than just words. Words — the content of communication — are one of three dimensions in which communication occurs.

Most of us are familiar with communication as content. Education that focuses on subject matter —the transmission of facts and information — is content based.

A second dimension of communication is process. Here, again, awareness of process skills is fairly common. Creative thinking and cooperative learning are examples of educational practices that focus on process as well as content.

The content is **what** you say, the process is **how** you say it.

The third dimension of communication — the context — goes unexamined even though the essence of the communication occurs here, since it includes the **who**, to **whom**, **when**, **where**, and **why** of the communication.

To take a statement "out of context" is to remove it from its original setting or frame of reference, thereby distorting its meaning. Virtually all miscommunication can be traced to differences in context. At my parent presentation, I spoke about self-esteem from my context and the parents heard what they heard in their contexts.

Purpose

The purpose of this activity is to help you reinforce the distinction among content, process and context, and gain practice in using awareness of context to improve communication.

Procedure

1. First complete the Worksheet: Content, Process, Context (page 78) before proceeding.

2. Select a controversial topic related to education; one that has at least two conflicting points of view, for example:

   - authentic assessment vs standardized tests

   - non-graded primary school

   - bilingual/multicultural education

   - full inclusion of special needs students

   - sex education

   - voucher system

   - prioritization of public schools

3. Write a one-paragraph position statement advocating one side of the argument, presenting the context in which the position makes sense.

4. Now, taking the opposite point of view, write another one-paragraph statement presenting the context validating this position.

5. Take the exercise one step further by finding common ground in the two opposing contexts. In terms of what both sides want for their children, is there any similarity in purpose? Anything to which both sides would agree is important?

See if you can create a new context that transcends the differing viewpoints and establishes alignment on common goals. (Note: Often it is the threat of a common enemy that has forced disparate groups to work together.)

CONTENT•PROCESS•CONTEXT WORKSHEET

Take the following list of words and write them under the heading indicating the dimension of communication to which they belong:

numbers	body language	graphs
medium	frame of reference	interpretation
words	facial expressions	speed of delivery
pictures	belief systems	expectations

CONTENT	PROCESS	CONTEXT
_____	_____	_____
_____	_____	_____
_____	_____	_____
_____	_____	_____

CONTENT•PROCESS•CONTEXT WORKSHEET

Answer Sheet

CONTENT	PROCESS	CONTEXT
numbers	body language	frame of reference
graphs	medium	interpretation
words	facial expressions	belief systems
pictures	speed of delivery	expectations

24 Listening for Context

Seek first to understand, then to be understood.
—Stephen Covey

Purpose

Author and consultant Tom Peters, in his groundbreaking work that brought excellence into the forefront of American business, interviewed a manager at a highly effective company who referred to "naive listening" as the secret to his success. Naive listening was defined as "listening as if I didn't know what the other person was about to say."

Japanese use the term "egoless" listening to refer to the same concept. In both cases what's being described is **listening for context** — listening to what someone else is saying and what it means to them. The process involves letting go of my frame of reference so that I can appreciate the context of the person delivering the communication.

The purpose of this activity is to give you practice in listening for context so that you can communicate in terms that will be most meaningful to the person with whom you are conversing.

Procedure

1. Identify someone with whom you disagree about an issue that's important to both of you.

2. Prepare a list of questions you could ask to help you understand his or her context. Keep in mind that a person's context is their "map of reality" comprised of beliefs, values, assumptions about self, others and life based upon:

   - childhood influences
   - family situation
   - religious upbringing
   - school experiences
   - work experience
   - age
   - gender
   - race, culture, language

- socio-economic status
- sexual orientation
- society's views of age, gender, race socio-economic status, and sexual orientation, and so forth.

3. Ask for an opportunity to meet with this person explaining that your purpose is to understand their point of view better so that you can work with them more effectively.

If the person is not available or not willing to meet with you, or if you are not comfortable having such a meeting, then do the exercise yourself — asking the questions you've identified and then answering them as best you can as if you were the other person.

25 Who R U?*

—Ruby Plenty Chiefs

Purpose

Sometimes the best way to get to a place of egoless listening is to
acknowledge your ego when it is doing your listening for you.

The ego is a point of view — usually coming out of a place of
fear and insecurity — that seeks to dominate, control, be superior
to, be right, avoid looking bad or losing.

See if you can recognize your ego in this exercise so that you
are better able to be responsible for it and consciously set it aside
when communicating.

Procedure

1. Read Column I: Communication Styles, on the Ego
   Manifestation Worksheet.

2. Match items in Column I with items in Column II by
   connecting the response in the Communication Scenario with
   the Communication Style it expresses.

3. For each of the three Communication Scenarios write a
   Principal Response you feel is more appropriate in terms of
   opening lines of communication and supporting the other
   person in solving his or her problem.

---

* This activity was adapted with permission from George M. Gazda et al., authors of *Human
Relations Development: A Manual for Educators* (Boston: Allyn and Bacon, 1984)

EGO MANIFESTATIONS WORKSHEET

COMMUNICATION STYLES

1. Detective

The Detective controls the conversation by focusing on the details of the case: "Just the facts, ma'am." The grilling style of questioning often puts the other person on the defensive.

2. Magician

The Magician tries to make the problem disappear by suggesting it isn't there. The other person often feels invalidated when his or her experience is discounted.

3. Foreman

The Foreman believes that the best way to help someone deal with a problem is to give them enough other work to do that they are too busy to worry about it.

This often leaves the other person feeling disregarded: that the work is more important than they are.

4. Hangman

The Hangman's job is to make the other person feel guilty by suggesting that he or she brought the problem upon themselves.

Having been punished rather than having been heard is often the result of this style.

5. Swami

The Swami prophesizes exactly what's going to happen in the future and gets to be right about it should the prediction come true.

This usually results in a no-win situation for the other person. If they take the Swami's advice, they do not get credit for the win. If they don't do what the Swami says, they get blamed for the loss.

COMMUNICATION SCENARIOS

Situation 1

A teacher comes to the principal seeking help with disciplining students. She complains that the children are out of control and she would like a stronger school-wide policy.

Principal Response A

"The children have a lot of energy they need to play out. They are all basically good kids who really want to behave. Most of the time they do an excellent job following the rules. I know someone as dedicated as you wants to make things even better. I'm sure after the vacation break, the students will calm down."

Principal Response B

"Just tell them to stop. Give them one warning and then send them to detention."

Principal Response C

"The students who give us problems are the hyperactive ones. Because of their Attention Deficiency Syndrome they just can't pay attention. Don't be a quitter. Learn to be more adaptive."

Situation 2

A parent calls the principal to express concern over a teacher's use of cooperative learning. He feels that his daughter is smarter than the other students and does most of the work, yet all the students in her group get the same grade.

Principal Response D

"Your daughter will accomplish great things. She will excel in whatever she does. You will be very proud of her. At this point in her life it is more important

83

6. Sign Painter

The Sign Painter thinks that by affixing a label you are actually fixing the problem.

Taking the behavior (complaining) and labeling the person (complainer) supposedly provides an explanation of the problem. The person is left feeling judged rather than supported.

7. Drill Sergeant

Drill Sergeants give commands and expect them to be obeyed: "And that's an order."

The other person feels that his or her opinions and feelings are of no consequence.

8. Guru

The Guru is a walking book of aphorisms with a trite cliché for every occasion.

Such generalities tend to trivialize the other person's concerns.

9. Florist

The Florist, seeking to avoid anything unpleasant, bestows flowery bouquets of optimism.

that she learn to work as part of a team. These social skills will be really important to her in whatever line of work she pursues."

Principal Response E

"Tell me exactly what your concerns are. What are the names of the other students who are not doing their part in the project? Have you spoken to her teacher?"

Principal Response F

"I'm so glad you called. I've been looking for parents who might be interested in serving on our School Improvement Council.

"You obviously care about the school and would be an excellent parent representatives."

Situation 3

A student is referred to the principal for consistent tardiness. The student explains family hardships make it difficult to arrive on time.

Principal Response G

"Getting to school on time is your responsibility. How do you ever expect to keep a job if you can't be punctual? You'll have to stay after school to make up the time."

Principal Response H

"Oh, come on now, it can't be that hard at home. I know children who live twice as far as you do and others who find time to do a paper route before school and still get here on time. You just have to do better."

Principal Response I

"You know the early bird gets the worm. Time is money. You're never too young to start learning good habits."

EGO MANIFESTATIONS WORKSHEET

Answer Guide

Situation 1
    Response A: Florist
    Response B: Drill Sergeant
    Response C: Sign Painter

Situation 2
    Response D: Swami
    Response E: Detective
    Response F: Foreman

Situation 3
    Response G: Hangman
    Response H: Magician
    Response I: Guru

26 Is Anybody Home?

> **O**nly men who are capable of truly saying thou to one another
> can truly say we with one another.
>
> —Martin Buber

Purpose

If I picked up a telephone and began speaking into it without having dialed a number, you would probably think it was bizarre behavior. In order to communicate via telephone, you need to get the person "on the line," you must be connected with your party.

The same principle operates in all communication — you must be connected.

This activity will give you some tips for how to establish and maintain rapport so that effective communication can occur.

Procedure

1. Read the guidelines on the Establishing and Maintaining Rapport Worksheet. Think of instances recently when you did or did not engage in each of these behaviors and how this affected the quality of your communication.

2. Each morning for the next week reread the list of guidelines to remind yourself to use them during the day.

3. At the end of the day, review the list again and check off any of the guidelines that you were conscious of using during the day.

4. At the end of the week, assess your progress. Note which skills are the easiest for you to remember and which ones you forgot most often.

5. Devise a plan for the next week to continue using these communication skills, paying special attention to those that need the most work.

ESTABLISHING AND MAINTAINING RAPPORT
WORKSHEET

- Greet the person in a friendly manner.

- Sit facing the person without desks or other barriers in the way.

- Maintain eye contact.

- Arrange not to be interrupted.

- Maintain an open, relaxed body posture.

- Stay attentive and focused.

- Know the purpose and intended result of the communication.

- Ask open-ended questions.

- Listen actively.

- Seek to re-create this person's frame of reference.

- Speak in language he or she understands using images, illustrations, metaphors to which he or she can relate.

- Pay attention to the volume, tone and tempo of your speaking in order to match your partner's communication style, modify your partner's communication style, and/or move the conversation toward achieving the intended result.

- Know when to remain silent and allow time for the other person to think and respond.

- Remember that speaking and listening are two different functions. Determine who is the speaker and who is the listener at any given time.

27 The Listener's Responsibility

The opposite of talking isn't listening.
The opposite of talking is waiting.

—Fran Lebowitz

Purpose

Delivering and receiving a communication are two distinct functions. It is important to know who is serving which function at any given moment.

Performing either function requires full responsibility. The listener, for example, is fully responsible for being open, attentive, intentionally working to grasp the meaning of the communication accurately. If miscommunication occurs, the listener must accept equal (i.e. 100%) responsibility for what didn't work.

You'll notice that equal responsibility on the listener's part in no way diminishes the responsibility of the person delivering the communication. He or she is also fully (100%) responsible for the success of the communication.

Procedure

1. Complete the I'm All EARS Worksheet by listing three examples — verbal or nonverbal — for each of the listening skills.

   For instance,
       ENCOURAGE
           Sit in close proximity.
           "Tell me more."
           "How did you feel about that?"

2. Review your schedule for the next week and select the most important meeting or appointment for each day. Draw a circle around each of these (an EAR ring?) to remind yourself to focus on these as opportunities to practice your listening skills.

3. Before each of these meetings review your EARS Worksheet to bring the skills back to mind. After the meeting, review the list again, and acknowledge yourself for being a good listener.

I'M ALL EARS WORKSHEET

Engage
_____
_____
_____

Ensure
_____
_____
_____

Encourage
_____
_____
_____

Attend
_____
_____
_____

Allow
_____
_____
_____

Acknowledge
_____
_____
_____

Restate
_____
_____
_____

Reflect
_____
_____
_____

Respond
_____
_____
_____

Support
_____
_____
_____

Summarize
_____
_____
_____

Suggest
_____
_____
_____

28 Meaning = Result

The true meaning of the communication is the result it produces.
—Author Unknown

Purpose

To be most effective, it is useful to accept full responsibility for your communications. If someone else misunderstands you, rather than assuming they weren't listening, accept the proposition that the correction can best be made in your delivery.

It seems to be human nature to want to find fault in someone else and to focus on trying to change other people's behavior. Your own behavior is much more in your control than someone else's. Accepting this level of responsibility empowers you to take action to improve things, whereas locating the problem outside yourself leaves you powerless.

Rather than thinking that the meaning of your communication lies in what you meant to say (i.e. what was in your head) operate from the premise that the true meaning of the communication lies in the **result** it produced. What happened in the world as a result of your communication? Were you effective in bringing about the outcome you intended?

— Did your assistant complete the report as you instructed?

— Were your constructive comments to your spouse received as supportive or critical?

— Was your absence at the meeting interpreted by your staff as an indication that you trusted them to do it without you, or that you didn't care enough to bother being there?

Procedure

1. On every written communication begin with a statement of the **purpose** and **intended result**. You may want to design a standard memo form with these headings and space to fill in statements so that it becomes institutionalized as a practice.

2. Be sure that all meetings have an agenda that spells out the purpose and intended result. Again, a standard form for this might be useful.

3. When agreeing to make an appointment to meet with someone, ask what their purpose and intended result is for meeting with you so that the time will be most productive.

4. Identify someone with whom you have difficulty communicating, have difficulty getting your point across, or getting what you need from them.

   Ask for support and counsel. Solicit suggestions they have for how you can be more effective in communicating with them.

   Follow their advice and monitor the results.

29 Powerfully Speaking*

Language is the road map of a culture. It tells you where its people come from and where they are going.

—Rita Mae Brown

Purpose

A kiss is just a kiss.

Well, that depends on what language you speak. German, I understand, has 30 different words, each describing a different type of kiss.

Words serve to make distinctions in how we perceive reality. Not only is seeing believing but also believing is seeing.

The Women's Movement clearly understood that women would remain unequal as long as the pronoun "he" was used to mean people in general, as long as companies were run by the "Chairman" of the Board, and as long as our Supreme Deity was referred to as "God the Father."

Educational research has demonstrated how labeling children affects how they are perceived by teachers. Specifically, one study showed that a child's behavior was rated appropriate or inappropriate depending on what special education term was used to explain the child's "condition."

This section offers strategies that support people in discovering greater power through their use of language. Certain words and phrases help us become aware of ourselves as being in control and able to take the necessary steps to reach desired outcomes. As we see new perspectives and new avenues for interpretation, our sense of ownership and responsibility is increased.

---

* Adapted with permission from Jack Canfield (co-author, *Chicken Soup for the Soul*). This activity originally appeared in *101 Ways to Develop Student Self-Esteem and Responsibility* by Jack Canfield and Frank Siccone (Boston: Allyn and Bacon, 1993)

Procedure

The following worksheet contains examples of how language can be used to shift from a disempowered (irresponsible) to an empowered (responsible) frame of mind, to move from feeling like a victim of circumstances to feeling capable and in charge.

Read the examples on the worksheet and fill in "responsible" examples on the spaces provided.

POWERFULLY SPEAKING WORKSHEET

Self as Source of Feelings

One of the most insidious and disempowering beliefs in our culture is that other people "make" us feel things. Outside of physically inflicted pain, no one else makes us feel hurt, sad, angry, upset, afraid, joyful, loved, or happy. It is simply not possible. "She makes me angry" is just as inaccurate as "You light up my life." We make ourselves feel certain ways by what we tell ourselves about other people, ourselves, and our circumstances.

Helping others accept responsibility for their feelings supports them in maintaining a healthy emotional state. This awareness also helps people realize the extent to which they are **not** responsible for hurting someone else's feelings. Although it is important to be sensitive to how others might react, it is liberating to know that everyone is ultimately responsible for his or her own experience.

Unempowered	"My boyfriend makes me so angry when he doesn't call me all the time."
Empowered	"The anger I feel is a result of my expectation that my boyfriend will call me every night even though I know he has other interests."
Unempowered	"My dad said that I really disappointed him when I didn't go into his line of work."
Empowered	_____ _____ _____

"I" Statements

Many times people will use the third person to talk about what they feel and think as if they are talking about someone else or "everybody." They may feel "safer," less on the spot, less likely to feel a need to defend their point of view. They are also not accepting responsibility for their thoughts and feelings. It is to their benefit to phrase their feelings and beliefs in the first person. Using "I" instead of "you" empowers individuals, and allows others to experience them as more sincere. What you think and feel is important both to you and others.

Unempowered	"When you do what you really want, you are happier."
Empowered	"When I do what I really want, I am happier."
Unempowered	"Everyone knows it's true."
Empowered	_____ _____ _____

From "ed" to "am ing"

Almost all feeling words that end in "-ed" describe conditions about ourselves that we are actually doing to ourselves — things over which we have control and can stop. Using such words robs us of our power, and makes it seem as if feelings and circumstances are victimizing us. When we change those same words to "am" and a word ending in "-ing," we take charge of our feelings and circumstances. For example:

Unempowered		Empowered
"I feel scared."	=	"I am scaring myself by imagining something bad will happen."
"I feel trapped."	=	_____ _____ _____
"I feel depressed."	=	_____ _____ _____
"I feel overwhelmed."	=	_____ _____ _____
"I feel confused."	=	_____ _____

"I feel frustrated."   =   _____
                                         _____
                                         _____
                                         _____

From Expectations to Intentions

Self-directed action, as opposed to waiting for someone else to do something, changes expectations to intentions. For example:

Unempowered   "I hope to get better grades this time."

Empowered   "I am studying harder now so that I can improve my grades."

Unempowered   "I wish the staff at my school got along better."

Empowered   _____
                    _____
                    _____

Trying Doesn't Do It

As with wishing and hoping, trying can be an indication of less than full confidence or commitment. For example, if someone asked to borrow a few thousand dollars from you and said he would try to pay you back, would you lend him the money? How about this situation? Your child had a serious illness that required that medication be given at a particular time. You asked the babysitter if she would remember to give the medicine at 7 P.M. and she said "I'll try." Would you entrust the life of your child to this person?

The higher the stakes, the less room there is for **trying** rather than **doing**. A clear intention to act is necessary for real success. While full commitment does not always guarantee success, it is certainly a more powerful way to approach a challenge than use of the word "trying" would suggest.

Unempowered   "I will try to give equal attention to all children."

Empowered	"I will use a system to help me keep track of the amount and type of attention I give each student."
Unempowered	"I'll try to remember to arrange for the field trip."
Empowered	_____ _____ _____

Being from Behavior

It is extremely helpful to distinguish my *being* (who I am) from my *behavior* (what I do). If I label myself "stupid," for example, it is much more difficult to change than if I view what I did as having been ineffective.

This is particularly important to remember when interacting with students. They feel bad after having received low grades because they judge themselves as bad people, not because of the grades themselves. School can be an emotional roller coaster for students if they don't learn that grades and evaluations are feedback on their work and not statements about their worth as human beings.

Unempowered	"I'm no good."
Empowered	"My skill in this area has not been developed very much."
Unempowered	"I'm clumsy."
Empowered	_____ _____ _____

From General to Specific

Generalizations, such as "always" and "never," are abstract concepts that lack the tangible base in reality that is necessary for change. Exaggeration and absolutes set up an atmosphere of helplessness and despair.

When we translate generalizations into specifics, we can begin to take action.

Unempowered   "Everyone hates me."

Empowered   "I'm having difficulty relating to my particular group of friends. Two of them said they don't want to hang out with me anymore."

Unempowered   "You are always late to class."

Empowered   _____
                  _____
                  _____

Unempowered   "I have too many students in my classes."

Empowered   _____
                  _____
                  _____

From Past to Present

People tend to believe that since something has happened in the past, it will *always* happen. Under this belief, change is not possible.

The past is the past. As history shows, if we keep repeating the same behavior, we will get the same results. If we change behavior, results change. Acknowledging the past and learning from it is important. The next step is to move forward into a future full of promise and possibilities. Students who learn that poor performance on one test does not seal their fate on subsequent exams have greater motivation to strive for success.

Speaking about undesirable or ineffective behavior as past history opens the possibility for change, for discovering new talents and developing new skills for greater success in the future.

Unempowered   "I always get nervous when speaking in front of groups."

Empowered   "Up until now, I've felt nervous when speaking in front of groups."

Unempowered	"I never know what to say to people who are negative all the time."
Empowered	_____ _____ _____

The Future to Present

When you have identified a positive change that you desire, you can use language to create the possibility of that change being immediate rather than "out there" in the future somewhere. The experience of being successful is available right now, and the potential for future success is only limited by your vision and willingness to commit to doing what will be necessary to realize this success.

Unempowered	"Someday, when I get a job that allows me more freedom, I'll be able to prove my worth."
Empowered	"I am constantly seeking opportunities in my current job to do exemplary work."
Unempowered	"After I've achieved my goal of losing 25 pounds, I'll feel good about myself."
Empowered	_____ _____ _____

From *If* to *When*

The purpose of the change in language from *if* to *when* is to enable us to be more successful in achieving our desired goals by shifting from something being possible or not (*if* it happens) to having it be a goal that is actually going to happen (it is just a matter of *when*).

Unempowered	"If only I could speak French."
Empowered	"When I am speaking French . . ."
Unempowered	"If only I could get parents to be more involved in their children's education."

Empowered   _____
                                _____
                                _____

Get Your 'But' Out of Here

When two people are sharing their respective perceptions or experiences, use of the article "and" allows for the possibility that two points of view can exist concurrently without being in conflict. The use of "but" however tends to negate one of the points of view, thereby disempowering the person whose view it is. "But" can also be used to build in an excuse. For example:

Disempowering   "I know you think I should be updating my curriculum, but I'm reluctant to change what I've been doing for 20 years."

This statement suggests that because the person is reluctant to change, the request to update is discounted.

Empowered   "I know you think I should be updating my curriculum and I'm reluctant to change what I've been doing for 20 years."

By using "and" instead of "but," the person is free to work on implementing the new ideas while also feeling reluctant to change.

Unempowering   "I believe that, in theory, all children are capable of succeeding in school, but some youngsters have way too many obstacles to overcome."

Empowered   _____
                 _____
                 _____

Chapter 4

Coaching

Coaching is face-to-face leadership that pulls together people with diverse backgrounds, talents, experiences and interests, encourages them to step up to responsibility and continue achievement, and treats them as full-scale partners and contributors.

—Tom Peters

Chapter 4   Coaching

Coaching is the process of enabling others to act, of building on their strengths. It's counting on other people to use their special skill and competence, and then giving them enough room and enough time to do it.

—Tom Peters

Introduction

Fortune magazine has predicted the end of jobs as we know them.

Before you head for your retirement home or the unemployment line, let me clarify.

A revolution is occurring in the workplace where jobs, title, positions, hierarchies, and so forth are becoming obsolete. Tomorrow's workers will function more independently, like entrepreneurs or one-person businesses. They will market their skills, work on a project-by-project basis and move from one work team to another.

Life-long learning will be essential since workers will need to be constantly upgrading their skills in order to keep up with new technologies and innovations.

In the new workplace, supervisors will be extinct. Workers will manage themselves. We are already seeing layers of middle managers being terminated as companies are restructuring and re-engineering their operations.

In place of supervisors, we will see project leaders and employee coaches. Project leaders will provide the direction for the team and the coaches will deal with motivation and the human side of the process.

The concept of manager as coach has already found its way into the vernacular, and training programs in this area are easy to locate.

How educational institutions will be affected by these changes remains to be seen. Whether the roles of teacher and administrator evolve in new ways is unknown. It does seem as if schools are looking to business for answers as critics become more vocal in decrying the failure of public education. Is restructuring this year's fad or does it hold the promise of really making a difference in how schools operate?

This section on coaching provides you with a series of structured interventions to help you enable your staff to succeed.

30 A Full 360 Degrees

I don't want any yes-men around me. I want everyone to tell me the truth — even though it costs him his job.

—Samuel Goldwyn

Purpose

This performance assessment is designed to help you identify the strengths you currently have as a coaching-style manager as well as those areas where you could improve your skills.

Gathering feedback from people who work with you on all sides — 360 degrees — is a way of providing you with as accurate a picture as possible.

Procedure

1. Make six copies of the Coaching Skills Inventory pages.

2. Complete one yourself.

3. Distribute the other copies to people who are familiar with your work habits — preferably your supervisor, one or more peers and up to three people whom you manage directly.

   Depending upon the level of comfort and trust that exists between you and your coworkers, you could have them return the forms directly to you with their names on it, return to you anonymously, or return to an independent third party for tabulation.

4. After the results of your coworkers are tabulated, compare their scores with yours to determine how consistently others perceive you compared to how you perceive yourself.

5. Note the items that received the three highest combined scores (your and theirs) and acknowledge yourself as being strong in these areas.

6. Identify the items that received the three lowest scores and develop plans to improve in these areas.

7. Repeat the process in six to twelve months to measure improvements.

COACHING SKILLS INVENTORY

To what extent do I engage in the following actions and behaviors?
Circle the number that applies to each statement.

	1 Rarely	2 Once in Awhile	3 Sometimes	4 Fairly Often	5 Very Frequently

LEADING VS. MANAGING

1. Demonstrate integrity, and base decisions and actions upon a consistent value system..................................... 1 2 3 4 5

2. Am visionary with a long-range perspective.................................... 1 2 3 4 5

3. Am innovative and challenge the status quo.. 1 2 3 4 5

4. Generate possibilities rather than limiting options...................................... 1 2 3 4 5

5. Set priorities — am effective (do the right thing) as well as efficient (do things right)... 1 2 3 4 5

6. Am proactive rather than reactive relative to goals...................................... 1 2 3 4 5

7. Think strategically — establish direction in terms of what needs to be done and let others determine how (tactics)................. 1 2 3 4 5

8. Favor direct action over bureaucratic systems... 1 2 3 4 5

9. Focus on people, not just on policies and procedures.. 1 2 3 4 5

10. Am passionate about education and generate enthusiasm in others................. 1 2 3 4 5

11. Inspire trust and commitment.................... 1 2 3 4 5

12. Promote warm human relationships rather than political intrigue.................. 1 2 3 4 5

1	2	3	4	5
Rarely	Once in Awhile	Sometimes	Fairly Often	Very Frequently

EMPOWERING

13. Exude confidence and personal power........ 1   2   3   4   5

14. Consistently manage with influence
rather than intimidation........................ 1   2   3   4   5

15. Am more likely to respond to a problem in
an appropriate manner, rather than
reacting in an overly emotional way......... 1   2   3   4   5

16. Am more interested in finding solutions,
rather than finding fault........................ 1   2   3   4   5

17. Am more focused on producing the result,
rather than gaining personal recognition.. 1   2   3   4   5

18. Spend more time supporting employees in
doing their work well, rather than trying
to find errors in their work..................... 1   2   3   4   5

19. Acknowledge others as contributors.......... 1   2   3   4   5

20. Help people find their own solutions to
problems, rather than telling them the
answer... 1   2   3   4   5

21. Give people feedback on their behavior
without putting them down...................... 1   2   3   4   5

22. Ask "what can we learn," when things
don't go as expected.............................. 1   2   3   4   5

23. Have the courage to admit having made a
mistake when something didn't work as I
planned... 1   2   3   4   5

24. Encourage feedback in order to adapt my
operating style..................................... 1   2   3   4   5

		1 Rarely	2 Once in Awhile	3 Sometimes	4 Fairly Often	5 Very Frequently		

COMMUNICATING 25. Encourage people to communicate fully and openly................................ 1 2 3 4 5

26. Seek to understand the meaning of what is being said.................................. 1 2 3 4 5

27. Listen to different points of view with an open mind................................ 1 2 3 4 5

28. Respect confidentiality............................ 1 2 3 4 5

COACHING AND COUNSELING 29. Listen to others in a non-judgmental manner.................................... 1 2 3 4 5

30. Am generally positive, supportive and encouraging.............................. 1 2 3 4 5

31. Am more likely to ask questions than to tell people what to do........................... 1 2 3 4 5

32. Ask questions that show sincere interest in the speaker.............................. 1 2 3 4 5

33. Ask questions that encourage honest responses rather than questions that get people to say what I want to hear............ 1 2 3 4 5

34. Ask questions that help people focus on what needs to be accomplished............... 1 2 3 4 5

35. Ask questions that challenge people to come up with creative solutions............... 1 2 3 4 5

36. Take the time necessary to make sure answers are complete and clear............... 1 2 3 4 5

37. Provide clear, useful feedback on projects.. 1 2 3 4 5

38. Am able to stay objective even in emotional situations.............................. 1 2 3 4 5

39. Treat people with respect and dignity — as individuals able to solve their own problems.............................. 1 2 3 4 5

1	2	3	4	5
Rarely	Once in Awhile	Sometimes	Fairly Often	Very Frequently

EDUCATING 40. Operate with a clear sense of purpose and mission.. 1 2 3 4 5

41. Set realistic goals................................. 1 2 3 4 5

42. Encourage others to set realistic goals....... 1 2 3 4 5

43. Willingly take time to provide important job information and training to employees.. 1 2 3 4 5

44. Articulate performance standards clearly... 1 2 3 4 5

45. Recognize and reward success.................. 1 2 3 4 5

SPONSORING 46. Am committed to the organization's goals and values.. 1 2 3 4 5

47. Show interest in other people's career development....................................... 1 2 3 4 5

48. Promote the success of people who work for me by keeping colleagues and superiors aware of their significant contributions.... 1 2 3 4 5

49. Work to eliminate barriers to employee performance....................................... 1 2 3 4 5

50. Work well with colleagues..................... 1 2 3 4 5

CONFRONTING 51. Am willing to face difficult situations directly... 1 2 3 4 5

52. Describe problems in a non-threatening tone and manner................................ 1 2 3 4 5

53. Am able to hold firm to a specified course of action.. 1 2 3 4 5

54. Hold people to their agreements in a non-accusatory manner................................ 1 2 3 4 5

55. Confront issues without being combative... 1 2 3 4 5

		1 Rarely		2 Once in Awhile	3 Sometimes	4 Fairly Often	5 Very Frequently		

TEAM BUILDING	56.	Encourage effective teamwork..................	1		2	3	4		5
	57.	Welcome leadership efforts from other team members..	1		2	3	4		5
	58.	Make sure that team mission and goals are understood......................................	1		2	3	4		5
	59.	Know when to make an independent decision and when group consensus is appropriate..	1		2	3	4		5
	60.	Effectively balance maintaining relationships with producing results........	1		2	3	4		5
	61.	Promote collaboration rather than competition..	1		2	3	4		5
	62.	Conduct effective meetings......................	1		2	3	4		5

31 Staff Assessment

If the only tool you have is a hammer, you tend to see every problem as a nail.

—Abraham Maslow

Purpose

In order to fulfill your responsibilities as a coach to your staff, it is helpful to know which coaching function most accurately describes your primary relationship with each person.

Procedure

Read through the Coaching Functions Overview as well as the Goals and Strategies of each of the separate Coaching Functions.

Next, fill out the Staff Assessment Worksheet by writing in the names of each person who you manage directly and then indicate which Coaching Function best characterizes the stage of your working relationship.

For example, if one of your teachers was just recently hired, you are probably still in the EDUCATING mode — helping them understand how the school operates, supporting them in getting to know their fellow teachers, providing suggestions on how to work with different aspects of the community, and so forth.

If your staff has just participated in an in-service workshop on cooperative learning, for example, you might serve in a COACHING capacity. Spending time in each classroom, your role is to encourage the teachers to try out some of the strategies, acknowledge their success, offer guidance when needed and model the skills being learned where appropriate.

As explained in the Overview, COUNSELING and CONFRONTING sessions are formal, structured meetings held in private.

SPONSORING and COLLABORATING will be addressed more fully in the section on Mentoring and in the chapter on Team Building.

COACHING FUNCTIONS

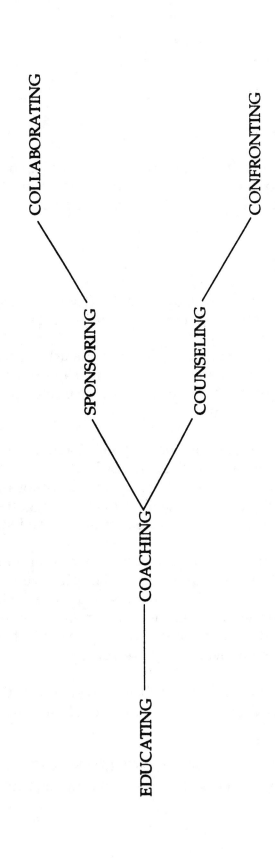

EDUCATING —— COACHING

SPONSORING

COLLABORATING

COUNSELING

CONFRONTING

COACHING FUNCTIONS
Overview

EDUCATING

As a manager, you have a responsibility to provide for the education and training needs of your staff. It is important that you assess what they know and what they don't know, and provide opportunities for them to increase their knowledge and skills.

Training may be done informally, on-the-job, or formally, through a structured program; and may include the following areas:

- teaching strategies needed to be effective with their school's student population

- the people skills needed to function with their fellow teachers

- knowledge of how the school is run

- information about the school district's culture and policies

- education about the community's values

COACHING

Coaching is a way of describing the on-going relationship you maintain with an employee once you both feel comfortable that adequate training has been provided. Most coaching occurs as a natural part of getting the work done. Sometimes it is appropriate to do a more structured coaching session.

Coaching should be a positive experience that provides either directional support — clarification of goals, alignment on priorities, helpful suggestions to improve work habits, etc.; or motivational support — acknowledgment, encouragement, identification of growth opportunities, etc.

113

COACHING FUNCTIONS
Overview - Continued

COUNSELING

Counseling is a more serious discussion related to a persistent performance issue that has not been corrected through coaching.

Counseling is most effective when:

- a formal coaching session has been held to address the issue with a warning that lack of improvement will result in a counseling session

- the employee knows that it is a counseling session that is being documented for inclusion in his/her personnel file

- both of you now agree what the problem is and how best to solve it

- the employee feels that you are sincerely interested in supporting his/her success

CONFRONTING

The term refers to confronting the issue not the person. A confronting session is a formal, structured conversation that represents at least the third time the issue at hand has been addressed — having had at least one or more coaching and one or more counseling sessions.

This is the employee's last chance to turn the situation around and correct the problem. The consequences of not doing so — whether it be reassignment, termination or whatever — ought to be clearly understood and in writing.

COACHING FUNCTIONS
Educating

GOALS

- Orient new employees

- Prepare new managers

- Provide for on-going training and development

- Encourage success within the school

- Establish direction

STRATEGIES

- Operate with a clear sense of purpose and mission

- Set realistic goals

- Encourage others to set realistic goals

- Take time to provide important job information and training to employees

- Articulate performance standards clearly

- Communicate school philosophy, values and operating principles

- Provide appropriate feedback and on-going support

- Create opportunities for on-the-job learning where risk is minimal

- Recognize and reward success

COACHING FUNCTIONS
Coaching

GOALS

- Empower success

- Maintain healthy relationships

- Encourage responsibility and commitment

- Promote standard of excellence

STRATEGIES

- Consistently manage with influence rather than intimidation

- Respond to a problem in an appropriate manner, rather than reacting in an emotional way

- Ask "what can we learn," when things don't go as expected

- Find solutions, rather than fault

- Focus on producing the result, rather than looking good

- Spend more time supporting employees in doing their work well, rather than trying to find errors in their work

- Acknowledge others as significant contributors

- Help people find their own solutions to problems, rather than telling them the answer

- Give people feedback on their behaviors without putting them down

- Have the courage to admit having made a mistake when something did not work as planned

- Reward innovation and calculated risk-taking

COACHING FUNCTIONS
Coaching

STRATEGIES - Continued

Listening

- Encourage people to communicate fully and openly

- Seek to understand the meaning of what is said

- Listen to different points of view without judging the speaker

- Respect confidentiality

- Engage in active listening techniques such as:

  Encourage
  Acknowledge
  Restate/Reflect
  Summarize

Questioning

- Ask questions that show sincere interest in the speaker

- Ask questions that encourage honest responses, rather than questions that get people to say what they think is expected

- Ask questions that help people focus on what needs to be accomplished

- Ask questions that do not encourage people to blame themselves or others for problems

- Ask questions that challenge people to come up with creative solutions

- Take the time necessary to make sure answers are complete and clear

COACHING FUNCTIONS
Sponsoring

GOALS	STRATEGIES
• Encourage autonomy	• Be committed to the organization's goals and values
• Reward creativity	• Show interest in other people's career development
• Retain excellent employees	• Promote the success of people by keeping colleagues and superiors aware of significant contributions
• Demonstrate by example	• Work to eliminate barriers to employee performance
	• Work well with colleagues
	• Provide access to information, people and opportunities
	• Allow an appropriate degree of autonomy
	• Emphasize long-term development in the context of school or district goals

COACHING FUNCTIONS
Collaborating

GOALS

- Establish a truly equal relationship not defined or limited by hierarchical lines of authority

- Enhance quality of results through peer coaching

- Increase awareness of "blind spots" and sabotage mechanism by having a trusted and committed partner

- Personal and professional growth

STRATEGIES

- Create opportunities to work together as partners on a project

- Discuss each other's strengths and areas for improvement

- Grant each other permission to serve as coach

- Establish a regular time to check-in on progress

- Provide feedback on how relationship is working

COACHING FUNCTIONS
Counseling

GOALS

- Improve performance

- Solve problems

- Reconfirm school values and performance standards

- Re-inspire commitment

STRATEGIES

- Be positive, supportive and encouraging

- Ask questions, rather than tell people what to do

- Listen to others in a non-judgmental manner

- Provide clear, useful feedback on projects

- Be specific about the area for improvement

- Define the intended result in objective and measurable terms

- Focus on an action plan for the future

- Stay objective even in emotional situations

- Treat people with respect and dignity — as individuals able to solve their own problems

- Recognize improvement and acknowledge turnaround

COACHING FUNCTIONS
Confronting

GOALS

- Deal with a serious situation or recurring problem

- Provide last chance for employee turnaround

- Consider reassignment or termination

STRATEGIES

- Face difficult situations directly

- Describe problems in a non-threatening tone and manner

- Focus on the correction that needs to be made

- Engage in joint problem solving

- Be prepared to suggest possible alternatives

- Allow feelings to be expressed

- Listen

- Elicit commitment to improve performance within a specific time frame

- Be extremely clear about the consequences if improvement does not occur

- Hold firm to a specified course of action

- Hold people to their agreements in a non-accusatory manner

- Confront issues without being combative

STAFF ASSESSMENT WORKSHEET

Person's Name   Coaching Function

_____   _____

_____   _____

_____   _____

_____   _____

_____   _____

_____   _____

_____   _____

```
                                                    COLLABORATING
                                                   /
                                    SPONSORING
                                   /
EDUCATING — COACHING
                                   \
                                    COUNSELING
                                              \
                                               CONFRONTING
```

32 Is It Worth It?

There are risks and costs to a programme of action. But they are far less than the long range risks and costs of comfortable inaction.

—John F. Kennedy

Purpose

Prior to conducting a formal COACHING session with a person to improve their job performance, it would be wise to conduct a Pre-Session Analysis to be certain that you have considered the implications of this intervention and feel that the commitment on your part will be worth the investment.

Procedure

Answer the following questions for yourself:

- Have I adequately fulfilled my responsibility for educating this person on his/her job specifications? If not, I need to educate before I can coach.

- Does the person know that his/her performance is not satisfactory? Have they been given adequate and constructive feedback?

- Does the person know what the results are supposed to be? Have they seen a demonstration lesson or in some other way been made aware of what is expected?

- Is the person **able** to do it? Does he/she have the knowledge, skills and resources necessary to do the job?

- Are there obstacles beyond his/her control? What have I done/can I do to help remove these?

- Is the person willing to do it? Is he/she motivated to do it?

- What are the consequences of good performance? (Are these perceived as positive or negative?)

- What are the consequences of poor performance? (Are these perceived as positive or negative?)

- Is it worth my time? Is it important enough? Will I make the time necessary to follow through on the process?

33 Being Prepared

Providence has hidden a charm in difficult undertakings which is appreciated only by those who dare to grapple with them.
—Anne-Sophie Swetchine

Purpose

If as a result of doing the Pre-Session Worksheet, you have decided to proceed with doing a COACHING session, then use this exercise to help you prepare.

Procedure

Complete the Coaching Process Worksheet.

COACHING PROCESS WORKSHEET

1. The purpose of this session is

❏   COACHING

❏   COUNSELING
when coaching has not produced the result

❏   CONFRONTING
when counseling has not produced the result

____Setting goals and priorities

____Solving a problem

____Following through on previous training

____Encouraging continued growth

____Presenting opportunities for greater responsibility

____Other

____Following up on lack of achievement of goals

____Improving performance substantially

____Resolving a persistent problem

____Dealing with morale problems

____Changing attitudes and behavior affecting the team

____Gaining renewed commitment to job and school

____Offering support and appropriate resources for problems of a personal nature

____Other

____Dealing with a serious situation

____Establishing deadline for recurring problem

____Explaining consequences of continued low performance or inappropriate behavior

____Providing last chance for turnaround

____Discussing reassignment or termination

____Other

2. My intended result is:

_____

_____

_____

_____

_____

COACHING PROCESS WORKSHEET -
Continued

3. Other possible outcomes might include:

    _____

    _____

    _____

    _____

4. The worst case scenario is:

    _____

    _____

    _____

    _____

5. The consequences if improvement doesn't occur will be:

    _____

    _____

    _____

    _____

6. The past history of this situation is:

    _____

    _____

    _____

    _____

7. Ways in which I may have contributed to this situation are:

    _____

    _____

    _____

    _____

COACHING PROCESS WORKSHEET -
Continued

8. What I could do differently in the future to support this person's success is:

_____

_____

_____

_____

9. What I think he/she could do differently in the future to improve the situation:

_____

_____

_____

_____

10. The best possible outcome for everyone concerned would be:

_____

_____

_____

_____

11. The number of meetings I think will be necessary to produce the result is:

_____

_____

_____

_____

12. In scheduling this session,

    the best date is: _____

    the best time is: _____

    the best location is: _____

34 Coaching to Improve Performance

The employer generally gets the employee he deserves.
—Sir Walter Gilbey

Purpose

The purpose of the COACHING session is to call attention to a specific aspect of the person's job performance in order to help him or her improve.

Many of the steps refer to skills presented in the previous section on communication.

Procedure

1. Review the Coaching Session Guidelines.

2. Conduct the actual session.

3. Complete the Coaching Session Self-Observation Sheet recording what actually happened and what you could do differently in the future to improve your coaching.

4. Monitor the situation, acknowledging progress as it occurs.

COACHING SESSION GUIDELINES

1. Establish **rapport**.

2. Indicate the **purpose** of the meeting.

3. State the **intended result** or **specific issue**.

4. Ask **open-ended questions** to solicit information about the other's perception.

5. **Listen** in an active manner.

6. Collaborate to define a **common goal** for the future.

7. Encourage identification of **possible solutions**.

8. Agree on best **course of action**.

9. Schedule **follow-up** session.

10. **Summarize** meeting detailing actions to be taken and time frame.

11. **Acknowledge** willingness to cooperate.

12. **Recognize** any achievement as it occurs.

COACHING SELF-OBSERVATION SHEET

1. Rapport was established   ❑ Yes   ❑ No
    What I actually said and did:

    Suggestions for improvement:

2. Purpose of the session was presented   ❑ Yes   ❑ No
    What I actually said:

    Suggestions for improvement:

3. Specific issue was stated   ❑ Yes   ❑ No
    What I actually said:

    Suggestions for improvement:

4. Open-ended questions were used   ❑ Yes   ❑ No
    What I actually asked:

    Suggestions for improvement:

5. Active listening skills were used   ❑ Yes   ❑ No
    Techniques actually used:
    ___Encouraging ___Restating/
              Reflecting
    ___Acknowledging ___Summarizing

    Suggestions for improvement:

COACHING SELF-OBSERVATION SHEET

6a. A common goal was established   ☐ Yes   ☐ No
    What was actually stated:

    Suggestions for improvement:

6b. Focus was on the future   ☐ Yes   ☐ No
    What I actually said:

    Suggestions for improvement:

7. Possible solutions were identified   ☐ Yes   ☐ No
   What was actually brainstormed:

   Suggestions for improvement:

8. Agreement was reached
   on the best course of action   ☐ Yes   ☐ No
   What actions were actually agreed on:

   Suggestions for improvement:

9. Follow up session was scheduled   ☐ Yes   ☐ No
   What date and time was set:

   Suggestions for improvement:

COACHING SELF-OBSERVATION SHEET

10. Meeting was summarized and a time frame was
    established   ❑ Yes   ❑ No

    What was actually said:

    Suggestions for improvement:

11. Session ended with positive acknowledgment   ❑ Yes   ❑ No
    What I actually said:

    Suggestions for improvement:

35 Counseling to Correct a Performance Problem

The strongest principle of growth lies in human choice.
—George Eliot

Purpose

Counseling — as mentioned in the overview — is only appropriate after one or more coaching sessions have been conducted.

You'll notice in reviewing the Counseling Session Guidelines that many of the steps are the same as in Coaching. Differences occur when the **open-ended questions** used in Coaching change to more **focused questions**, and the idea of a goal shifts to discussing the issue as a **problem**.

The key to a successful Counseling Session is to get an agreement on the existence of the problem and a commitment on the person's part to correct it.

A serious Counseling Session might be documented for inclusion in the person's personnel file. (A sample form is included.) You would want to check with the legal advisor in your district (County, State, etc.) to be sure that this procedure is consistent with the union contract in effect in your organization.

Procedure

1. Review the Counseling Session Guidelines.

2. Conduct the actual session.

3. Complete the Counseling Self-Observation Sheet recording what actually happened and what you could do in the future to improve your coaching.

4. Monitor the situation, recognizing improvements as they occur.

5. Conduct the follow-up session. If the desired improvement has occurred, acknowledge the person for their commitment. Continue to move the relationship in a positive direction.

   If the desired improvement has not occurred, discuss what the next steps are — another Counseling Session or a Confronting Session. Explain the consequences of these.

COUNSELING SESSION GUIDELINES

1. Establish **rapport**.

2. Indicate the **purpose** of the meeting.
   (Mention documentation and use the documentation form if appropriate.)

3. State the **specific issue**.

4. Ask **focused questions** to accomplish the next three steps.

5. Get **agreement** on the problem.

6. Collaborate on identifying **possible solutions** that focus on the employee's responsibility.

7. Select a mutually agreeable **course of action**.

8. Confirm the employee's **commitment** to taking these actions to solve the problem.

9. Establish a short-term **follow-up** checkpoint.

10. **Summarize** the discussion.

11. **Acknowledge** the employee's commitment to resolving this issue.

12. **Recognize** any achievement as it occurs.

COUNSELING   DOCUMENTATION FORM

Employee:_____

Supervisor:_____

Date:_____

Purpose of Session: _____

_____

_____

_____

Specific Issue Addressed: _____

_____

_____

_____

Agreed-Upon Action Plan: _____

_____

_____

_____

Date of Follow-Up Evaluation: _____

Employee Commitment:
I understand that my performance in this area has been a problem and I agree to improve the situation by implementing the action plan we've identified.

_____   _____
Employee's Signature   Supervisor's Signature

FOLLOW-UP EVALUATION:

Employee has: Surpassed Expectations ❑
                    Met Expectations   ❑
                    Not Met Expectations ❑

Next Steps:

_____

_____

_____

_____

_____

_____

_____

_____   _____
Employee's Signature   **Supervisor's Signature**

_____   _____
Date   Date

COUNSELING SELF-OBSERVATION SHEET

1. Rapport was established   ❏ Yes   ❏ No
    What I actually said and did:

    Suggestions for improvement:

2. Purpose of the session was presented   ❏ Yes   ❏ No
    What I actually said:

    Suggestions for improvement:

3. Specific issue was stated   ❏ Yes   ❏ No
    What I actually said:

    Suggestions for improvement:

4. Focused questions were used   ❏ Yes   ❏ No
    What I actually asked:

    Suggestions for improvement:

5. Agreement on the problem was reached   ❏ Yes   ❏ No
    How the problem was stated:

    Suggestions for improvement:

COUNSELING SELF-OBSERVATION SHEET

6. Possible solutions were identified   ❏ Yes   ❏ No
   What solutions were suggested:

   Suggestions for improvement:

7. Mutual agreement   ❏ Yes   ❏ No
   on action plan was reached
   What was actually agreed to:

   Suggestions for improvement:

8. Commitment was confirmed   ❏ Yes   ❏ No
   What he/she actually said:

   Suggestions for improvement:

9. Follow-up checkpoint was scheduled   ❏ Yes   ❏ No
   What date and time was set:

   Suggestions for improvement:

10. Meeting was summarized   ❏ Yes   ❏ No
    What was actually said:

    Suggestions for improvement:

COUNSELING SELF-OBSERVATION SHEET

11. **Employee was acknowledged**   ❑ Yes   ❑ No
     What I actually said:

     Suggestions for improvement:

36 Confronting the Issue to Produce Turnaround

There is no fruit which is not bitter before it is ripe.
—Publilius Syrus

Purpose

In this procedure, you are confronting the issue not the person and you are doing so in a professional, rational manner rather than in an emotional way which the term confronting sometimes conveys.

A Confronting Session is only appropriate as a final step after a series of Coaching and Counseling Sessions have failed to resolve a particular issue.

A Confronting Session should be documented as a follow-up to the documentation done at a previous Counseling Session. (A sample form is provided.) Once again, you should check with your district, county or state's legal counsel to be certain that this procedure complies with contractual regulations. Since you will be discussing the consequences involved if the situation isn't corrected, you'll need to know what your options are available — legally — and contractually.

The point to stress when doing a Confronting Session is that now there are two problems — the original performance issue about which you've been coaching and the added fact that an agreement was broken. Emphasize that in order for you to be able to work with someone, you need to know that they will keep their word; that when an agreement is made, it will be kept. Without this as a foundation, there is no basis for a working relationship.

Procedure

1. Review the Confronting Session Guidelines.

2. Conduct the actual session.

3. Complete the Self-Observation Sheet.

4. File the appropriate documentation. Monitor the situation closely. Recognize any improvement that occurs.

5. Conduct the follow-up session. If improvement occurs continue to work toward moving the relationship in a positive direction.

   If improvement does not occur, follow through on consequences that were discussed.

CONFRONTING VS. CRITICIZING

I praise loudly, I blame softly.

Catherine the Great

CONFRONTING	CRITICIZING
Addresses the **problem**	Blames the **person**
Seeks to find **solutions**	Seeks to find **fault**
Focuses on **specifics**	Diffuses into **generalizations**
Occurs in context of **relationship** (Win/Win)	Occurs in context of **me against you** (Win/Win)

CONFRONTING SESSION GUIDELINES

1. Establish **rapport**.

2. Ask: "Do you know the **purpose** of this meeting?

3. Confirm the **specific issue**.

4. Ask: "What has **happened** in this area?"
    "What **progress** has been made?" etc.

5. Ask: "What **agreements** did you make in this area?"
    "What is the agreed-upon **performance standard**?" etc. (Refer to
    documentation form.)

6. **Summarize** previous two points (e.g. "So, you agreed to . . . and
    you didn't do it?")

7. Ask: "Did you keep your **agreement**?"
    "Did you do what you said you would?"

8. Ask: "If you do not do what you say you are going to do, what
    basis do we have for an **employment relationship**?"

9. Be certain that he or she understands the **impact** of this situation
    on him/her, other team members, you, and the organization.
    Reinforce the point that the real problem now is that you can
    only work with people who deliver on what they say.

10. Discuss what **options** remain at this point.

11. Decide upon the most appropriate **course of action**.

12. Be clear and direct about what needs to happen and the
    consequences if turnaround doesn't occur.

13. Establish a short-term **follow-up** meeting.

14. **Summarize** the session. Fill out and sign the documentation
    form.

15. Conclude the session with a sincere expression of **support**.

CONFRONTING   DOCUMENTATION FORM

Employee:_____

Supervisor:_____

Date:_____

Specific Issue Addressed: _____

_____

_____

_____

Date(s) of Previous Counseling on this Issue: _____

_____

What must be done now to correct this situation? _____

_____

_____

_____

What are the consequences if improvement does not occur? _____

_____

_____

What is the time frame for improvement? _____

_____

Employee Commitment:
I understand that this is my last opportunity to resolve this issue. I know what I need to do to improve it and what the consequences will be if I don't.

_____   _____
       Employee's Signature   Supervisor's Signature

FOLLOW-UP EVALUATION:

❑   Yes, this issue has been resolved satisfactorily.
❑   No, this issue has not been resolved satisfactorily.

Next Steps:

_____

_____

_____

_____

_____

_____

_____	_____
Employee's Signature	Supervisor's Signature
_____	_____
Date	Date

CONFRONTING SELF-OBSERVATION SHEET

1. Rapport was established   ❑ Yes   ❑ No
    What I actually said and did:

    Suggestions for improvement:

2. Purpose of the session was reviewed   ❑ Yes   ❑ No
    What I actually said:

    Suggestions for improvement:

3. Specific issue was confirmed   ❑ Yes   ❑ No
    What I actually said:

    Suggestions for improvement:

4. Status check of progress was made   ❑ Yes   ❑ No
    What I actually asked:

    Suggestions for improvement:

5. Prior agreements and agreed-upon performance   ❑ Yes   ❑ No
    standards were reviewed
    What I actually asked:

    Suggestions for improvement:

CONFRONTING SELF-OBSERVATION SHEET

6. Progress and agreements were summarized ☐ Yes ☐ No
    What was actually said

    Suggestions for improvement:

7. Fulfillment of agreement was questioned ☐ Yes ☐ No
    What I actually asked:

    Suggestions for improvement:

8. Basis for relationship was raised
    What I actually said: ☐ Yes ☐ No

    Suggestions for improvement:

9. Impact of this situation was discussed
    What I actually said: ☐ Yes ☐ No

    Suggestions for improvement:

10. Options were considered
    What was actually discussed: ☐ Yes ☐ No

    Suggestions for improvement:

CONFRONTING SELF-OBSERVATION SHEET

11. Course of action was decided upon   ❑   Yes   ❑   No
    What was actually agreed to:

    Suggestions for improvement:

12. Consequences were clearly established   ❑   Yes   ❑   No
    What was actually discussed:

    Suggestions for improvement:

13. Short-term follow-up meeting was scheduled   ❑   Yes   ❑   No
    What date and time was set:

    Suggestions for improvement:

14. Session was summarized and documentation form   ❑   Yes   ❑   No
    completed
    What was actually said:

    Suggestions for improvement:

CONFRONTING SELF-OBSERVATION SHEET

15. Support and acknowledgment were given at close   ❑ Yes   ❑ No
    of session
    What I actually said:

    Suggestions for improvement:

Part III

Leadership of Others Too:
Facilitating Teams

A leader articulates a vision and persuades people that they want to become part of it, so that they willingly, even enthusiastically, accept the distress that accompanies its realization.

          —Michael Hammer and James Champy

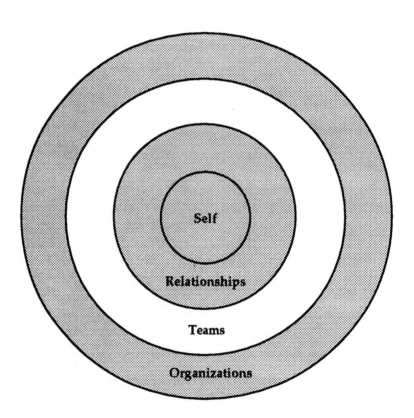

Part Three Leadership of Others Too: Facilitating Teams

*Innovation creates opportunity;
quality creates demand;
but teamwork makes it happen!*

—James B. Miller

Introduction

Teams have emerged as the decade's most important organizational tool for increasing productivity. This trend has emerged in educational institutions as well, where site-based management and cooperative learning have become commonplace.

Whether you think of a football team or an orchestra, when a group of individuals adopt a collective identity toward achieving a common goal then a synergy is created that is very powerful. What more significant common goal could there be than the education of our children?

This section of the book details how to facilitate team building including how to avoid typical pitfalls.

A chapter on Running Effective Meetings will be cheered by your staff as meeting time is reduced and productivity increased.

Collaborative approaches to decision making, problem solving and conflict resolution complete the sequence.

If you've ever been associated with a group that had a high degree of team spirit, you can appreciate the energy, excitement and effectiveness that's possible.

Chapter 5

Team Building

My intention always has been to arrive at human contact without enforcing authority. A musician, after all, is not a military officer. What matters most is human contact. The great mystery of music making requires real friendship among those who work together. Every member of the orchestra knows I am with him and her in my heart.

—Carlo Marie Giulini
Conductor
Los Angeles Philharmonic

Chapter 5 Team Building

Introduction

When a group of individuals come together to form a team they tend to progress through four developmental stages:

- **Forming**

  The initial phase when people tend to be on their best behavior, waiting to see how the group members interact.

- **Storming**

  This is when friction occurs around issues of control. Power struggles are common and disagreements about how the group is to function need to be settled.

- **Transforming**

  When a goup successfully navigates through the storming stage it emerges as a more cohesive unit. The process for resolving conflict through communication and collaboration transforms the group of individuals into a more unified team.

- **Performing**

  The final stage is when the team becomes highly productive and concerns about group process become secondary. High levels of mutual respect and trust are characteristic of teams at this level.

The four stages of team building are outlined further in the following pages. The activities in this chapter are designed to help you facilitate your team through these phases, resulting in enhanced relationships and improved results.

STAGES OF TEAM BUILDING

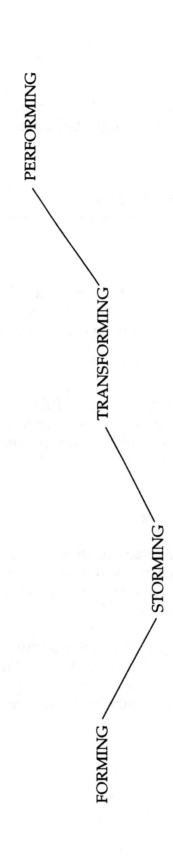

FORMING — STORMING — TRANSFORMING — PERFORMING

156

TEAMBUILDING
Stage One: Forming

GOALS

- Establish rapport among members

- Define team purpose/mission and vision

- Establish team goals and objectives

- Acknowledge importance of each person's contribution

STRATEGIES

- Provide time for individual introductions

- Ask each member to consider: "What do I want to contribute to this group?", and "What do I want the group to contribute to me?"

- Discuss expectations regarding
  - the result to be produced
  - the challenges of the task
  - the group process

- Support the group in staying focused, recognizing that irrelevant topics are likely to surface as part of the process of defining roles and boundaries

TEAMBUILDING
Stage Two: Storming

GOALS

- Create context for this phase being part of the process

- Encourage responsible communication

- Promote collaboration rather than competition

- Neutralize affects of power struggles, tension and jealousy

- Resolve issues of control

STRATEGIES

- Discuss "Storming" as a natural phase of teambuilding

- Suggest group members describe their experience of having been on other teams

- Brainstorm ways of supporting effective group process

- Use structured teambuilding activities to help the group process through this phase

- Establish a structure for dealing with issues related to group process

TEAMBUILDING
Stage Three: Transforming

GOALS

- Develop team "Operating Instructions," agreements or ground rules

- Operate with effective methods of problem solving and decision making

- Establish each member's personal responsibility for commitment to the team's success — results and relationships, product and process

- Shift from being a group of individuals to a cohesive team with a common goal

STRATEGIES

- Acknowledge what's working and what's not working for the group

- Discuss need for getting organized

- Engage team in process of developing and agreeing to "Operating Instructions"

- Insist on responsible communication and active listening

- Alternate responsibility for team facilitation and encourage leadership efforts from other team members

- Demonstrate team success by moving ideas into action, achieving objectives

TEAMBUILDING
Stage Four: Performing

GOALS

- Produce results

- Experience feelings of strong bonds, mutual support, positive regard

- Realize team's contribution to the organization

STRATEGIES

- Recognize individual strengths and allow these to be contributed to overall team effectiveness

- Celebrate accomplishment of objectives toward achievement of larger goals and team purpose

- Acknowledge successful resolution of issues as they arise

- Merchandise team's contributions

37 Team vs Group of Individuals

No member of a crew is praised for the rugged individuality of his rowing.

—Ralph Waldo Emerson

Purpose

While many people may have worked within groups, served on committees and so forth, there is something distinctly different about a team — especially a high performance team.

The point of this activity is to help the people in your group make that distinction so they can be more responsible for their role in functioning as an effective team.

Procedure

1. Set up two flip charts or two layers of butcher paper.

2. Ask the group to brainstorm the difference between a "group of individuals" and a high performance "team." Record their comments on the respective flip charts.

3. When everyone has had a chance to list as many characteristics as they can to distinguish between group and team, let them know that it is your intention to work together with them to take advantage of the positive attributes of being a team.

4. Continue with the next activity now or save the flip chart pages for the next opportunity the group has to meet.

38 Characteristics of an Effective Team

Never one thing and seldom one person can make for a success. It takes a number of them merging into one perfect whole.
—Marie Dressler

Purpose

To have your team appreciate what it takes for a group to function as an effective team.

Procedure

1. Post the brainstormed list of items generated during the previous activity using the pages from the "team" side.

2. Tell the group that you want them to select the items from these pages that are relevant to them as a team. The brainstorming may have elicited some team characteristics that relate to sports, for example, which may not be applicable to a team of school administrators or a school staff.

3. Review the list, asking which characteristics are relevant. Leave on the list those that the group feel are appropriate and cross off the ones that don't apply.

   Allow for discussion to occur. In cases where unanimous opinion does not exist, as long as one or more members of the team feel an item belongs, leave it on the list, at least for now.

4. As a final check, let the group know that you are going to use the Characteristics of an Effective Team as the basis for assessing how well this team functions. Review the list from this viewpoint and agree on how many team performance measures to have and which ones are most important.

39 Assessing Team Performance

You don't get the breaks unless you play with the team instead of against it.

—Lou Gehrig

Purpose

In order to enhance team functioning, your group will rate itself on how well it performs against certain agreed-upon criteria. This same assessment tool can be used on an on-going basis at regular intervals.

Procedure

1. Using the Characteristics of an Effective Team agreed upon during the last activity, inform the team that they will be rating how well they have been functioning up until now.

2. Using a five-point scale — 1) Almost never, 2) Seldom, 3) About half the time, 4) Frequently, 5) Almost always — go around the group having each person call out the number that reflects how he or she feels the team has been performing on each of the characteristics. Record these on the easel pages next to each of the characteristics.

3. Next, determine the average rating of each characteristic.

4. Focusing first on the high scores, acknowledge these as Team Strengths and allow for discussion of examples.

5. Now, discuss the low scores and invite the group to comment.

6. In cases where there is a wide range of scores, ask the group to explore the implications of this.

7. Finally, let the team know that they will be developing team goals and that this base-line data will prove useful for that purpose.

40 Give and Take

When you cease to make a contribution you begin to die.
—Eleanor Roosevelt

Purpose

It is important that people be allowed to contribute their interests, strengths and talents to the team so that they feel valued.

It is equally important that people feel that they are receiving value back from their involvement so that they feel their contribution is being reciprocated.

When people feel unable to contribute, they feel disenfranchised, and when they are not being contributed to, they feel resentful.

Procedure

1. Hand out copies of the Give and Take Worksheet.

2. Have people find a partner. Each person interviews the other using the questions on the worksheet.

   There are a number of ways of dividing the group into pairs. Some ideas are:

   - Get together with the person you know least on the team.

   - Pair up with the person whose birthday (month and day) is closest to yours.

   - Find someone else who, like yourself, was the first born, last born, middle child or only child.

3. Allow the pairs about ten minutes for the interviews, five minutes each. Halfway through the allotted time, let them know that if they haven't already switched they should do so.

4. At the end of the time for interviews, invite the pairs to come together again as a full team. Have each partner report on what he or she found out about the person they interviewed.

5. Allow for full group discussion about the activity, what they learned about themselves and about the motivation of their teammates.

GIVE AND TAKE WORKSHEET

1. What do you most want to contribute as a member of this team? What knowledge, experience, skills, and talents can you offer in support of the team's efforts?

   _____

   _____

   _____

   _____

   _____

   _____

   _____

   _____

   _____

   _____

2. What do you want to receive in return for your contributions? How could you benefit from being on the team? What could you gain from the experience?

   _____

   _____

   _____

   _____

   _____

   _____

   _____

   _____

   _____

   _____

41 Team Communication

Seek first to understand, then to be understood.

—Stephen Covey

Purpose

Communication is one of the single most important skills required for team success.

Through this activity, your staff will be reminded of the importance of active listening.

Procedure

1. Hand out copies of the AAA Active Listening Worksheet and have the group brainstorm examples — verbal and nonverbal — of active listening skills.

2. Divide the group into teams of seven or eight people, and ask each team to select a process observer. The process observer's role is to ensure that active listening skills are being used. He or she will not get involved in the discussion.

3. Distribute the Have a Heart Worksheet and review the instructions. Emphasize that before anyone offers an opinion he or she must have **A**llowed time for the previous speaker to finish, **A**ccept what the other person has said as being a valid point of view, and **A**cknowledge that person's contribution to the discussion.

   The process observer is responsible for making sure this happens and will stop the discussion when necessary to request that this rule be followed.

4. At the end of the twenty minutes ask each process observer to report what happened in his or her group.

5. Open the discussion to the full group, and invite comments regarding the implications of this experience to their continued work as a team.

AAA ACTIVE LISTENING WORKSHEET

ALLOW

	Verbal	Non Verbal
Example:	"Please tell me what you think."	Open posture

_____	_____
_____	_____
_____	_____
_____	_____

ACCEPT

	Verbal	Non Verbal
Example:	"I understand your point of view."	Head nodding

_____	_____
_____	_____
_____	_____
_____	_____

ACKNOWLEDGE

	Verbal	Non Verbal
Example:	"Thank you for contributing your ideas."	Eye contact

_____	_____
_____	_____
_____	_____
_____	_____

HAVE A HEART WORKSHEET*

Imagine that you are a group of surgeons at a big hospital. As a committee you must make a very important decision. There is one heart donor at this time, and there are eight patients who need a heart transplant. So far as we know, the prognosis for a successful transplant is the same for all the patients. Your committee must decide who will receive the transplant. You have 20 minutes to arrive at a group consensus.

PATIENTS

1. A 17 year-old Chicana waitress. She is a high school dropout and the sole provider for her family.

2. A 15 year-old pregnant woman. She is unmarried, white and has no other children.

3. An Hispanic high school senior, class president, who recently won a scholarship to medical school.

4. A 24 year-old single mother with three young children. A Vietnamese who has no other family in this country.

5. A 52 year-old African American religious leader who runs a homeless shelter and soup kitchen that feeds thousands of people daily.

6. A 40 year-old scientist close to discovering a cure for AIDS. He is a white male who is HIV positive himself.

7. An 11 year-old Middle Eastern girl who has become a symbol for world peace.

8. A transfer patient from a small rural medical facility. Other data not available.

---

* Adapted with permission from *Training High School Conflict Managers*, p. SF-9 (Revised, 1996) by The Community Board Program, 1540 Market St., Ste. 490, San Francisco, CA 94102

42 Team Trust

How ow can the people trust the harvest, unless they see it sown.
—Mary Renault

Purpose

Trust is another one of those fundamental conditions for team performance. Without trust, little progress can be made.

This activity asks team members to define the concept of trust in behavioral terms, and to communicate with one another what is required for trust to exist as part of the team's culture.

Procedure

1. Hand out copies of the Team Trust Worksheet.

2. Have team members write out their answers to questions 1, 2 and 3.

3. With the group sitting around in a circle, have each person read the answers to these questions.

4. Having heard the requests from their teammates, ask each person to answer question 4 on the worksheet.

5. Now, once again, go around the circle with each person reading his or her commitment to the team.

TEAM TRUST WORKSHEET

1. I feel most trusted when

    _____

    _____

    _____

2. I feel least trusted when

    _____

    _____

    _____

3. In support of creating team trust, I request

    _____

    _____

    _____

4. In support of creating team trust, I commit to

    _____

    _____

    _____

43 Get to Know Me

It is a fault to wish to be understood before we have made ourselves clear to ourselves.

—Simone Weil

Purpose

This activity helps team members get to know each other better. Metaphorical symbols are used to reveal different aspects of a person's nature.

The process is based on a model that suggests that human beings have three layers of self:

1. Outer Self — Persona/Personality
   Who I think I am or who I want you to think I am.

2. Intermediate Self — Fear
   Who I am afraid I am or who I am afraid you will think I am.

3. Inner Self — Essence
   Who I really am

Some people find difficulty with the level of creative thinking involved as well as with the degree of self-disclosure required. Be prepared for forms of resistance to appear during the exercise. Persevere, for the results are worth it.

Materials

Each participant will need 3 boxes — a small 4"x 4", medium 5"x 5" and large 6"x 6" size so that they fit one inside the other, and a few marking pens (permanent ink is best so it doesn't rub off on people's hands).

Procedure

1. Hand out markers and the largest of the three boxes.

Give the following instructions to the team:

"Reserving the top of the box for last, please draw a picture on one of the side panels of the vacation spot that best describes your communication style." (Allow about 5 minutes for each item throughout the activity.)

"Now on a second side panel, please draw a picture of an animal that best describes your work habits."

"On a third side panel draw a composer, musician, singer or group that best characterizes your personality."

"On the fourth side panel, an historical figure that best characterizes your leadership style."

"Now on the top cover of this box draw a picture of a product — a package good or something that might be advertised on TV, for example — that best captures how you want this team to think of you."

2. Ask the group to set aside this box, letting them know they will have an opportunity to share their drawings with the team later. Hand out the middle size boxes.

3. Give the following instructions:

"Again, saving the top of the box for last, please use one of the sides of the box to do your drawing in response to . . . (Follow the same procedure for the remainder of these items.)

"An item on a restaurant menu that best symbolizes how you feel when you are under a lot of stress."

"Book or movie title that captures how you deal with conflict."

"Toy, game or sport that characterizes a fear you have in being part of this team."

"Dream or nightmare depicting your greatest personal fear."

"On the top of the box write a tabloid newspaper headline related to what you are afraid this group will think about you."

4. Instruct everyone to put this middle size box inside the larger box and set them aside until later. Pass out the small box and continue with the process.

"On one of the side panels please draw an image representing a holiday that characterizes one of you core values."

"On another side panel write the motto by which you try to live your life."

"Thirdly, something in your house that symbolizes a fundamental belief you have."

"On the fourth side, a drawing of a time, place or person where you feel most loved and loving."

"Finally, on the top of this box — a word or image that could appear on your tombstone expressing who you really are."

5. When everyone is finished, have them put the small box inside the other two, and bring the group together in a circle. If the group is large, you can divide them into smaller groups or carry out the procedure over the course of a number of sessions.

6. Ask for a volunteer to start, and have this person share the images and what they mean on the outer box only.

7. When this first person is finished, he or she calls the name of someone else on the team who will go next. Continue in this manner until everyone has shared their outer box.

8. Repeat the same procedure with the middle box and again with the inner box.

9. To complete the process, invite members of the team to share their experiences of going through it, what they learned about themselves and each other.

44 Learning from Past Experience

*E*xperience is not what happens to a man:
it is what a man does with what happens to him.

—Aldous Huxley

Purpose

This activity validates people's past experience as the basis for building future success.

Most everyone has been on one kind of a team or another. Whether these experiences were positive or not, they can serve to teach what works about being a "winning" team and what doesn't.

Procedure

1. Hand out the Learning from Past Experience Worksheet.

2. Give people a few minutes to fill out the worksheet for themselves.

3. Go around the group and have each person share his or her answers to the questions on the worksheet.

4. Using two flip charts or sheets of butcher paper, record "What Works" on one side and "What Doesn't Work" on the other in order to capture the collective wisdom of this group's experience.

    These notes can be typed and distributed to team members for future reference. They could also serve as the basis for developing Team Agreements (Activity 49).

LEARNING FROM PAST EXPERIENCE WORKSHEET

The **best** experience I ever had on a team:

_____

_____

_____

What I **learned** from that experience that can be applied to this team:

_____

_____

_____

The **worst** experience I ever had on a team:

_____

_____

_____

What I **learned** from that experience that can be applied to this team:

_____

_____

_____

45 Stormy Weather

The world is wide, and I will not waste my life in friction when it could be turned into momentum.

—Frances Willard

Purpose

For the team to realize that conflict — storming — is a natural part of the process of team development so that they can be prepared for using these as opportunities to transform the group into a high performance team.

Procedure

1. Hand out the Stormy Weather Worksheet.

2. Have the group divide itself into subteams of four to six people. There are a number of ways of accomplishing this such as:

   - Ask the group to count off one to four, five or six (depending on the size of the group). All the "ones" get together to form a subteam, "twos," "threes" and so forth.

   - Bring together the same pairs from Give and Take (Activity 40) and have each couple find a pair in order to make a group of four (or three pairs to form teams of six).

   - Using a deck of playing cards, deal one card to each person, then have all like cards get together to form a team of "four of a kind" (four aces, four sixes, and so forth).

3. In their subteams, have them discuss conflicts they have experienced using the questions on the worksheet to guide the discussion. Assign each group the task of summarizing their findings into a group of recommendations that they would like the full group to adopt.

Allow sufficient time for the subteams to discuss the questions and prepare their recommendations.

4. Bring the full group together. Have a reporter from each subteam present their group's findings.

   Having each subgroup put their recommendations on butcher paper is an efficient way of managing the process.

5. Combine the recommendations from each of the subgroups into one final list for the full team's adoption.

   Start by agreeing on the common points from all the groups.

   If there are recommendations that appear on some lists and not all, find out if everyone is comfortable with keeping them on the final list or if the group that suggested the item is willing to eliminate it.

   Any conflicts that arise are perfect opportunities for the team to learn how to deal with each other. Refer to the list of common recommendations for guidance on how to deal with the areas of conflict.

6. Complete the activity by having the group come to consensus on the conflict-resolution strategies they will use in the future.

STORMY WEATHER WORKSHEET

1. What types of conflicts have you seen occur among teams?

   _____

   _____

   _____

   _____

2. How did the team react to these conflicts?

   _____

   _____

   _____

   _____

3. What do you think were the issues underlying the conflicts?

   _____

   _____

   _____

   _____

4. Were these underlying issues ever resolved to everyone's satisfaction?

   _____

   _____

   _____

   _____

5. What recommendations do you have for how this team should deal with conflicts such as these should they arise?

   _____

   _____

   _____

   _____

46   Team Balance

Our team is well balanced. We have problems everywhere.
—Tommy Prothro

Purpose

One of the areas where teams often find themselves in conflict is how much time to spend on process (team relationships) versus getting on with the job (team results).

Some people are more task oriented than others and become impatient when the team gets bogged down in procedure. Others, however, want to avoid making rash decisions and need more time to process the issue.

This activity is meant to encourage team members to be sensitive to the needs of others and adjust their own style in support of team success.

Procedure

1. Draw a larger version of the Team Balance chart on the board or easel pad.

2. Distribute copies of the Team Balance Worksheet I and ask them to complete the questionnaire and tally their score.

3. Have markers available and instruct team members to put their initials on the chart in the quadrant indicated by their score on the questionnaire.

4. Have a brief discussion with the group as to how they feel about their personal scores and what the implications are for the team.

5. Next, ask the team to divide themselves into two groups based upon which quadrant they are in, and have each group get together in opposite corners of the room.

6. Hand out copies of the Team Balance Worksheet II and have the two teams fill out their forms within their teams.

7. Have one person from each of the teams report on how his or her group answered the questions.

8. Open up the discussion to the full group for any final comments.

TEAM BALANCE CHART

③ HIGH RELATIONSHIPS LOW RESULTS	④ HIGH RELATIONSHIPS HIGH RESULTS
① LOW RELATIONSHIPS LOW RESULTS	② LOW RELATIONSHIPS HIGH RESULTS

TEAM RELATIONSHIPS (vertical axis)

TEAM RESULTS (horizontal axis)

TEAM BALANCE WORKSHEET I

Rate your preference for each of the following items by giving it a score of 0 to 5 (0 means low preference, 5 is high preference). The scores for each pair must add up to 5 (0 and 5, 1 and 4, 2 and 3, and so forth).

____ 1a.   The best part of being on a team is that the results are enhanced by more people working together.

____ 1b.   The best part of being on a team is that the process is more interesting given the different personalities.

____ 2a.   I prefer the efficiency of making decisions myself.

____ 2b.   I prefer involving others in the decision-making process because I think it leads to better informed decisions.

____ 3a.   I am most productive when working in a group situation.

____ 3b.   I am most productive when working alone.

____ 4a.   Meeting deadlines is critical, and people need to adjust their pace accordingly.

____ 4b.   Timelines should be able to be adjusted if they interfere with people's work styles.

____ 5a.   Feedback is most meaningful to me when it is focused on how I can work better with others.

____ 5b.   Feedback is most meaningful to me when it is focused on how I can perform my assigned tasks better.

____ 6a.   When I choose others to work with me, I look for an ability to work with other people and concern for the team.

____ 6b.   When I choose others to work with me, I look for a track record of results.

____ 7a.   The future success of this organization depends on people.

____ 7b.   The future success of this organization depends on productivity.

____ 8a. One of my weaknesses as a communicator is overlooking people's feelings.

____ 8b. One of my weaknesses as a communicator is losing sight of the end result.

____ 9a. I motivate others by recognizing individual productivity.

____ 9b. I motivate others by reminding them of their importance to the team.

____ 10a. At the end of the day I feel the greatest satisfaction when I have gotten a lot accomplished.

____ 10b. At the end of the day I feel the greatest satisfaction when I have had positive interactions with members of my team.

TEAM BALANCE SCORING SHEET

Transfer your scores for each item to the appropriate blanks. Add each column to determine the total for the Relationships and Result dimensions. Plot your score on the chart below.

1b._____	1a._____
2b._____	2a._____
3a._____	3b._____
4b._____	4a._____
5a._____	5b._____
6a._____	6b._____
7a._____	7b._____
8b._____	8a._____
9b._____	9a._____
10b._____	10a._____

Total Relationships_____ Total Results _____

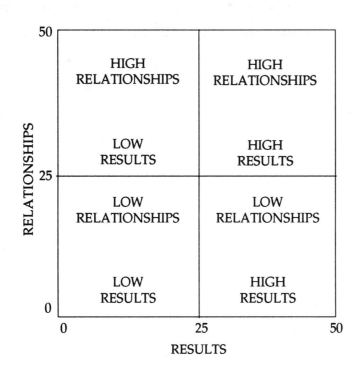

TEAM BALANCE WORKSHEET II

1. We would characterize our strengths as

   _____

   _____

   _____

2. Given our strengths, we can contribute to the team by

   _____

   _____

   _____

3. Our teammates on the other side of the room might say we need to improve our skills in

   _____

   _____

   _____

4. Our teammates on the other side of the room could help us by

   _____

   _____

   _____

47 Team Mission

Pick battles big enough to matter, small enough to win.
—Jonathan Kozol

Purpose

One major difference between a fully effective team and a group of individuals is that teams usually have a sense of purpose or mission — a common direction toward which they are working together.

Procedure

1. Hand out copies of the Team Mission Worksheet.

2. Ask each person to complete the worksheet defining what he or she feels is the team's mission.

3. When the individuals are finished, have them find a partner. Partners share their Team Mission Statement with one another and then work together to come with one statement between the two of them. The combined statement should be an integration of the views of both partners.

4. Next, have each pair get together with another pair. The couples share the Mission Statement they developed while in pairs and then as a foursome work to integrate these two statements into one with which all four team members concur.

5. Continue the process in this manner so that the groups of four become eight, eight become sixteen and so forth until a full team Mission Statement has evolved.

6. Complete the activity with an opportunity for people to discuss the process and the resulting Mission Statement.

TEAM MISSION WORKSHEET

1. What contribution is this team looking to make? (Skills, talents, strengths, and so forth.)

   _____

   _____

   _____

2. To whom or in what arena will the team's contribution be made? (Intended recipients, target audience, area of involvement, and so forth.)

   _____

   _____

   _____

3. What end result will be the outcome of the team's contributions? (Vision, positive benefits, improved conditions, and so forth.)

   _____

   _____

   _____

TEAM MISSION STATEMENT

Now combine your answer to the three questions into one statement.

_____

_____

_____

_____

48 Team Goals

Without some goal and some efforts to reach it, no man can live.

—Fyodor Dostoevsky

Purpose

A mission statement is used to set the team's direction, goals serve to focus the team's efforts on concrete accomplishments.

Involving team members in setting goals helps build a sense of ownership for the team's success, and as goals are achieved, team members will experience a greater sense of efficacy and empowerment.

Procedure

1. Post the team's Mission Statement as well as the Ground Rules for Brainstorming.

2. Introduce the activity by indicating the purpose being to define what the team wants to achieve this year.

3. Review the Ground Rules for Brainstorming.

4. Ask the question, "What goals do we intend to accomplish this year related to or as an expression of our Mission?" Invite the team to brainstorm as many ideas as possible.

5. Record all the ideas on flip charts for everyone to see.

6. Encourage everyone to participate. You may want to challenge the group to come up with a certain number of activities within a designated amount of time, such as twenty ideas in ten minutes.

7. After the brainstorming session, have the team applaud themselves in acknowledgment of their creativity.

8. Now it is time to select which of these goals the team will actually work to accomplish. Have all the flip chart pages posted so all the ideas are visible. Provide markers and invite

each team member to put a check next to the idea he or she would like to see the team adopt as their priority.

9. Discuss with the team how many goals they could realistically accomplish given their other commitments, limitations of time and resources, and so forth.

   If there is an obvious first choice, ask if everyone is willing to accept this goal as the team's priority.

   If a number of goals were chosen for consideration, allow a certain amount of discussion to compare the advantages and disadvantages of the various options. Everyone on the team could once again select their choice from the three or four possibilities.

10. After the team has selected at least one priority goal, use the SMART guidelines (Activity 6) to help the team refine the goal.

GROUND RULES FOR BRAINSTORMING

- Everyone contributes as many ideas as possible.

- Piggy-backing on other's ideas is fine.

- There are no good or bad ideas when brainstorming.

- Innovative, unusual, outrageous, off-the-wall ideas are welcome.

- Discussing the ideas and evaluating their usefulness will be deferred until later.

49 Team Agreements

People support what they help to create.

—Anonymous

Purpose

The purpose of this activity is to bring to a conscious level how individual behavior can enhance or detract from team functioning. Having team members create their own ground rules promotes greater responsibility for the team's well being.

Procedure

1. Introduce the activity by stating that the purpose is for the team to create a healthy work environment for itself, and hand out copies of the Team Agreements Worksheet.

2. Following procedure similar to the Team Mission (Activity 47) have each team member first write down what he or she requires to feel comfortable participating as a member of the team. A list of examples are provided.

3. After an appropriate amount of time, have each individual find a partner and as a pair collaborate on one list to which both parties agree. Continue the process by having the pairs form teams of four, foursomes becomes teams of eight, and so forth until the entire team has worked together to produce one list.

4. Have the final list of Team Agreements posted each time the team meets.

TEAM AGREEMENTS — EXAMPLES

- Listen when someone else is speaking.

- Treat everyone with respect.

- If you have a problem with someone in the team, address it with the person directly.

- Seek to find solutions rather than finding fault.

- All meetings will start and end on time.

- Respect different perspectives and handle disagreements in a constructive manner.

TEAM AGREEMENTS WORKSHEET

1. INDIVIDUAL GROUND RULES

    In order to create an environment in which I would feel comfortable participating fully, I recommend the following ground rules:

    _____

    _____

    _____

    _____

    _____

2. SUBGROUP GROUND RULES

    In order for the team to be effective, we recommend the following ground rules:

    _____

    _____

    _____

    _____

    _____

3. TEAM AGREEMENTS

    In support of team process and productivity, we as a team agree to the following ground rules:

    _____

    _____

    _____

    _____

    _____

50 Project Teams

It is a bad plan that admits of no modification.

—Publilius Syrus

Purpose

The team's goals (Activity 48) will only be achieved if individual team members accept responsibility for completing certain tasks that together will culminate in the attainment of the desired goal.

In this activity, project teams are established to work on various aspects of the team's goals.

Procedure

1. Starting with the Team's Goal(s), ask the group to identify the various projects that make up the goal.

    For example, if the goal is to increase computer literacy among students, projects might include in-service training for teachers, a parent involvement group, a school business alliance plan, a peer tutoring program, and so forth.

2. Ask team members to volunteer to work on one of the project teams.

3. Hand out copies of the worksheets Characteristics of Project Teams and Project Team Brief. Have the project teams meet to discuss their project and complete the Briefing form.

4. Bring the entire team together and ask each team leader to report on their project team's process.

5. Project teams are to provide progress reports to the full team on a regular basis.

CHARACTERISTICS OF PROJECT TEAMS

- Project teams are empowered and accountable for the results.

- Project teams are self-managed. Coaches may be requested or assigned on the basis of their ability to add value.

- Project teams are interdisciplinary and may include "clients" as well as outside "experts" where appropriate.

- Project teams select their own leader. Leadership of the team may rotate to other team members during the course of the project.

- Project teams are not committees. They are action oriented and disband once they have produced the result.

- Traditional titles and positions do not apply.

PROJECT TEAM BRIEF

TEAM   _____

GOAL   _____
                  _____

TITLE OF
THIS PROJECT   _____
                  _____

PROJECT TEAM MEMBERS

_____   _____
_____   _____
_____   _____

TEAM LEADER   _____

PROJECT OBJECTIVES:

_____
_____
_____
_____

ACTION PLAN:

WHAT	WHO	WHEN
_____	_____	_____
_____	_____	_____
_____	_____	_____
_____	_____	_____
_____	_____	_____
_____	_____	_____
_____	_____	_____
_____	_____	_____
_____	_____	_____
_____	_____	_____
_____	_____	_____
_____	_____	_____

51 Team Performance Evaluation

When the going gets tough, everyone leaves.

—Lynch's Law

Purpose

In this activity team members assess how well they have been performing relative to their Mission and Team Agreements. It encourages team members to work together in being responsible for maintaining an effective team environment.

Procedure

1. Fill in the Team Mission and Team Agreements (Activity 47 and 49).

2. Duplicate the worksheet and distribute copies to the team.

3. Ask team members to rate how well they and the team have been doing in keeping their agreements.

4. Instruct them to write down what they and the team can do to improve their effectiveness.

5. Start with those areas where the team has been most successful by asking for the items that received the highest scores. Acknowledge these.

6. Then focus on the areas that received the lowest scores. Discuss ways in which team effectiveness could be improved in these areas.

7. Be open to revising the team agreements if necessary.

8. Have each team member state individually what he or she intends to do to continue to improve team effectiveness.

TEAM PERFORMANCE WORKSHEET

Rate the team performance on a scale of 1 to 5.

1	2	3	4	5
Poor	Adequate	Good	Very Good	Excellent

1. To what extent do you feel the team is fulfilling its mission?

Team Mission

_____

_____

_____

_____

2. To what extent do you think the team is keeping its agreements? Also, how would you rate your own performance?

Team Agreements	Team Rating	Personal Rating
_____	_____	_____
_____	_____	_____
_____	_____	_____
_____	_____	_____
_____	_____	_____
_____	_____	_____

3. What recommendations do you have for improving team effectiveness?

_____

_____

4. What can you do personally to contribute to the team being more effective?

_____

_____

52 In the Loop

*People forget how fast you did a job
— but they remember how well you did it.*

—Howard W. Newton

Purpose

In order for the team to improve their performance on a continual basis, team members need to be willing and able to give (and receive) feedback to each other. A feedback loop allows for mid-course corrections, adjustments and refinements.

This activity is designed to help team members feel more comfortable in giving and receiving feedback by establishing guidelines for making the process positive and productive.

Procedure

1. Start by building a case for the importance of team feedback. Put the words "COSTS" and "BENEFITS" on a board or large piece of paper, and ask the group to brainstorm the benefits of being able to give and receive feedback (positive feedback as well as suggestions for how the team and/or individual team members could work together better).

   Then brainstorm possible costs. (People feeling hurt, becoming defensive, refusing to participate further, are examples.)

2. Next, tell the group that the purpose of this exercise is to maximize the benefits and minimize the costs, and hand out copies of the Giving and Receiving Feedback Worksheet.

3. Invite everyone to complete the answers on their worksheet. Sample guidelines are provided to stimulate their thinking.

4. Bring the group together in a circle or in small groups if the team is large and the time is limited, and have them read their guidelines (Answer to Question 8).

5. After one of the Team Performance Assessments, encourage team members to meet in pairs to give each other feedback using the guidelines they established.

GIVING AND RECEIVING
FEEDBACK WORKSHEET

1. Describe a time when you received feedback you found truly beneficial.

   _____

   _____

   _____

   _____

   _____

   _____

   _____

2. What was there about what was said (content), how it was said (process), and the conditions (context) that made it effective?

   _____

   _____

   _____

   _____

   _____

   _____

3. Describe a time when you received feedback you felt was destructive or of no real value.

   _____

   _____

   _____

   _____

4. What made it ineffective?

   _____

   _____

   _____

   _____

5. What conclusion about giving feedback can you draw from your experience?

    _____

    _____

    _____

    _____

    _____

6. What conclusion about receiving feedback can you draw from your experience?

    _____

    _____

    _____

    _____

    _____

7. What obstacles get in the way of giving and receiving feedback?

    _____

    _____

    _____

    _____

    _____

8. What guidelines for giving and receiving feedback would you propose?

    _____

    _____

    _____

    _____

    _____

GUIDELINES FOR GIVING FEEDBACK

- Be clear that your purpose for giving feedback is to **support** the other person by offering input that he/she will find valuable. This is not the time for you to release your frustrations or make the other person wrong.

- Select an **appropriate** time and place.

- Get **permission** to offer input.

- Establish the **context** for the communication — speak about the purpose and **refer** to the overall relationship, including positive aspects, before discussing the area for improvement.

- **Own** what you say as you personal opinion.

- Focus on **behavior** rather than the person — addressing areas that the person is able to control or change.

- Make **observations**, not interpretations — descriptions, not judgments.

- Be **specific.**

- Be **sensitive** to how your communication is being received and how much the person is able to hear.

- Offer **suggestions** and recommendations with an orientation toward the future.

- Allow the other person to respond, and **listen** to what he/she says.

- Be sure that the communication is complete. **Acknowledge** the other person for being willing to receive feedback.

Chapter 6

Effective Meetings

Meetings ... are rather like cocktail parties.
You don't want to go, but you're cross not to be asked.

—Jilly Cooper

Chapter 6   Effective Meetings

The most successful managers are those who will see their fundamental work not as making decisions, but as making mutual understanding.

—Peter Schwartz

Introduction

Not Another Meeting?

Check your appointment book. What percentage of your time do you spend in meetings — staff meetings, parent conferences, principal's council, superintendent's cabinet, school board meetings?

The purpose of this section is to give you tools to make meetings more productive so that you not only get more done in the meetings but you also free up more time away from meetings so you can accomplish some of your goals.

53 To Meet or Not To Meet?

Meetings are indispensable when you don't want to do anything.

—John Kenneth Galbraith

Purpose

One way of making meetings more effective is to have fewer of them. If you can accomplish your purpose without one, go for it. Everyone would appreciate having to meet only when there is a compelling reason for doing so.

Procedure

Before scheduling a meeting, complete the following checklist.

I am scheduling a meeting because:

- ❏ It is the most efficient way of sharing information

- ❏ I want the entire group to receive the information or discuss an issue at the same time

- ❏ I want to involve the group in solving a problem

- ❏ I want to involve the group in making a decision

- ❏ A problem exists and it is unclear what the source of the problem is or who is responsible for it

- ❏ Confusion exists around an issue that involves everyone

- ❏ The group itself requests a meeting

- ❏ There is a problem that involves people from different groups

- ❏ I want to build a sense of team

I have decided not to schedule a meeting because:

- ❑ It is better to communicate one on one, by telephone or by memo

- ❑ The subject is trivial

- ❑ The subject is confidential (such as personnel issues)

- ❑ There is too much anger in the group and they need time to calm down first

- ❑ All the key members cannot attend

- ❑ Group members are preoccupied with more pressing issues

- ❑ It would be meeting just for the sake of meeting

54 A Time to Every Purpose

I am a great believer, if you have a meeting, in knowing where you want to come out before you start the meeting. Excuse me if that doesn't sound very democratic.

—Nelson Rockefeller

Purpose

The efficiency of a meeting correlates directly with how clear people are on the purpose and intended results.

Procedure

As you prepare for your next meeting review the list of possible purposes and results, and then write your statement of purpose and intended result(s).

POSSIBLE PURPOSES

- To share information

- To gather information

- To solicit input and opinions

- To build consensus around a decision

- To solve a problem

- To influence people's thinking

- To motivate people to act

- To build and maintain a sense of team

- To establish a direction, set goals and plan of action

- To expand awareness

- To develop skills

PURPOSE STATEMENT

The purpose of this meeting is to:

_____

_____

_____

_____

POSSIBLE RESULTS

- A written document recording the facts and information gathered

- Minutes of the meeting recording people's opinions on the topics discussed

- A decision that everyone understands, and is able and willing to support

- Agreement on the source of a problem

- Brainstormed list of many possible solutions to a given situation

- Agreement on the best possible solution

- A procedure for how similar situations will be handled in the future

- A majority of the group votes in favor of the resolution

- A third of the group enrolls into the program

- A set of team agreements are identified

- A Strategic Plan is developed

RESULTS STATEMENT

The intended result(s) of this meeting is/are:

_____

_____

_____

_____

TYPES OF MEETINGS

INFORMATIONAL   (CONTENT)

- Share information, present facts

- Discuss topic, answer questions, solicit feedback

INTERACTIVE / TRANSACTIONAL   (PROCESS)

- Develop a plan

- Solve a problem

- Make a decision

TRANSFORMATIONAL   (CONTEXT)

- Motivate to act

- Educate or train

- Build a team

211

55   What's On the Agenda?

The length of a meeting rises with the square of the number of people present

—Eileen Shanahan

Purpose

Having an agenda is a way of keeping a meeting focused and controlling the use of time.

The point of this exercise is to help you know when to use an agenda and how to put one together.

Once you've identified the purpose and intended result(s) of the meeting, you can determine if an agenda would support the process.

Generally speaking, there are three types of meetings: informational, interactive or transactional and transformational.

- An **informational** meeting is usually characterized by one-way communication. Information is presented by one person to the group. Sometimes a brief question and answer/discussion period is allowed.

  An agenda is most helpful in these types of meetings. A number of business items can be covered in a short period of time. Background information can be sent out in advance of the meeting so that group members can be prepared with pertinent questions.

- An **interactive** or **transactional** meeting is really a working session designed to allow sufficient time for full discussion of issues. Expression of various points of view is encouraged increasing confidence that decisions are being made based on adequate exploration of the facts and implications.

  An agenda may or may not be helpful since you may not be able to estimate how much interaction will be required for the group to arrive at a solution. A good facilitator, however, can mean the difference between a successful meeting and a disaster.

- A **transformational** meeting is a session intended to produce dramatic change in people's experience of themselves and/or the group. Management training simulations and outdoor adventure team-building exercises are examples of transformational meetings.

  Once again, a facilitator — probably an outside consultant — is going to prove more critical than an agenda.

Procedure

Using the Agenda Format provided, prepare an agenda for an upcoming informational meeting. Consider what items need to be included, who will be responsible for presenting each item and how much time will be allowed.

Some of my clients build in time at the beginning of the meeting for the group to review the agenda and decide the order based on priority importance. Another group of school administrators who are monitoring their meeting behavior also leave time at the end to discuss how well the meeting went — what worked and what can be improved next time.

AGENDA FORMAT

PURPOSE
OF MEETING   _____

_____

_____

INTENDED
RESULT(S)   • _____

• _____

• _____

AGENDA

WHAT	WHO	HOW LONG
_____	_____	_____
_____	_____	_____
_____	_____	_____
_____	_____	_____
_____	_____	_____
_____	_____	_____

AGENDA FORMAT   (SAMPLE)

PURPOSE
OF MEETING   To keep the Management Team informed on
                    issues that involve the entire district.

INTENDED
RESULTS

- Answer questions that have arisen since last meeting regarding new state regulations

- Be sure everyone is informed of in-service training schedule

- Generate a list of names of potential speakers for mid-year district-wide staff development workshop

AGENDA

WHAT	WHO	HOW LONG
Review agenda and prioritize	Superintendent	5 minutes
Discuss new state regulations and address questions	Director of Special Services	20 minutes
Distribute in-service training calendar	Staff Development Coordinator	5 minutes
Brainstorm names of potential speakers	Staff Development Coordinator	5 minutes

56 Pass the Deal

If you must play, decide upon three things at the start: the rules of the game, the stakes, and the quitting time.
—Chinese Proverb

Purpose

Interactive meetings tend to work best when they are structured with clear roles for a facilitator, recorder and group members. Since the facilitator yields a certain amount of power over the group process, it is often a good idea to have the facilitator role rotate among the members of the group. This allows for the power as well as the responsibility for the group's success to be shared. Someone who knows that he or she will be facilitating next week's meeting is more likely to be supportive of this week's facilitator.

An additional benefit to rotating facilitators is that it gives an opportunity for everyone in the group to develop their facilitation skills. This becomes important when identifying the appropriate person to facilitate a particular topic since the facilitator must be someone who can remain neutral: someone who is focused on group process not on the content of the discussion. Having everyone prepared as facilitators increases the likelihood of having someone who is able to manage a particular agenda item.

Procedure

1. Prepare a set of cards that are blank on one side and have one of the meeting roles (facilitator, recorder, group member) on the other. You can do this by duplicating the descriptions on the following pages. You'll need enough group member cards for all but two people — the facilitator and the recorder.

2. At your next staff meeting discuss the idea of having a rotating facilitator and recorder, and review the job functions of each role.

3. Put the cards down in the center of the table and have each group member select a card to determine who will facilitate and record for this meeting.

4. At the end of the meeting, debrief the process by asking the facilitator and recorder to share what they liked about how they did their jobs, and also what they learned that they would like to pass on to future facilitators and recorders.

   Next, invite the group to acknowledge first what worked for them about the meeting, and secondly, what they learned that they will use when it is their turn to record or facilitate.

5. Bring out the cards again, and give a "group member" card to this meeting's facilitator and recorder so they will not repeat these roles until everyone else has had a turn.

   Shuffle the deck and ask each member of the group to pick one to determine who will facilitate and record at the next meeting.

6. Repeat this process at each subsequent meeting.

ROLES

ROLE OF FACILITATOR	• Keeps the group focused on the process
	• Encourages participation from everyone
	• Listens, accepts and validates everything that is said without judgment
	• Makes suggestions about the process
	• Makes sure the recorder is able to keep up
	• Asks someone to keep track of the time
	• Does not contribute his/her own ideas about the topic

ROLE OF RECORDER	• Writes what is being said on newsprint or butcher paper so that everyone can read it
	• Uses key words and phrases from group members
	• Invites the group to let him or her know if something is recorded inaccurately
	• Does not contribute his or her own ideas regarding the topic

ROLE OF GROUP MEMBER	• Contributes ideas
	• Supports the process
	• Listens to and respects other's ideas
	• Honors time limits

57 Meetings Wrap Up

I said what is very true, that any committee is only as good as the most knowledgeable, determined and vigorous person on it. There must be somebody who provides the flame.

—Lady Bird Johnson

Purpose

The purpose of this activity is to provide you with an easy reference for continually improving the effectiveness of your meetings.

Procedure

Before your next meeting — and all subsequent meetings — answer the questions on this checklist.

EFFECTIVE MEETINGS CHECKLIST

- What is the **purpose** of the meeting?

  _____
  _____
  _____

- What specific **outcome** do you want to achieve?

  _____
  _____

- Is there a **more effective way** of accomplishing the same purpose and outcome?
  - ☐ Yes   Then do it.
  - ☐ No   Then schedule the meeting.

- If a meeting is appropriate, **who** needs to attend?

  _____
  _____
  _____

- What information do they need **prior** to the meeting in order for the intended outcome to be produced?

  _____
  _____
  _____

- What **actions** will occur during the meeting in order to achieve the outcome?

  _____
  _____
  _____

- What is the appropriate **sequence** of events?

  _____
  _____
  _____

- How much **time** will be needed for the meeting?

  _____

- Will you prepare an **agenda**?
  - ❑ Yes
  - ❑ No

- What **handouts, materials, supplies** will you need?
  _____
  _____
  _____

- **Where** will the meeting be held?
  _____

- What **room set up** will best support your purpose?
  _____

- What **problems**, if any, do you anticipate might arise during the meeting?
  _____
  _____
  _____

- What could you do **beforehand** to address these concerns?
  _____
  _____
  _____

- Who is the best person to **lead** the meeting, given the purpose of it?
  _____

- Would having an impartial **facilitator** support the purpose?
  - ❑ Yes   Who? _____
  - ❑ No

- Would having a **recorder** to take notes be useful?
  - ❑ Yes   Who? _____
  - ❑ No

Chapter 7

Decision Making
and
Problem Solving

I find that the three major administrative problems on a campus are sex for the students, athletics for the alumni, and parking for the faculty.

—Clark Kerr

58 How You Decide Is As Important As What*

You'll never have all the information you need to make a decision. If you did, it would be a foregone conclusion, not a decision.

—David J. Mahoney, Jr.

Purpose

How you make a decision can be as important as the decision you make.

Some people prefer to be in control and are most comfortable making a decision themselves in a top-down, unilateral manner. While this may be efficient, it runs the risk of the decision not being as informed as it would have been had other people's input been solicited. Also, the implementation of the decision may be problematic due to people's not feeling included in the process.

On the other hand, a more participatory style may take an inordinate amount of time to ensure everyone's included — and there still is no guarantee that they will ever agree.

The point of this activity is that there is no one right way to make a decision; it depends upon the situation.

Procedure

1. Review the eight different decision making styles presented here along with factors to consider in selecting the style that is most appropriate.

2. Complete the Decision Making Worksheet using an actual decision that you need to make sometime in the near future.

---

* Adapted with permission from *Mastering Meetings for Results* (San Francisco: Interaction Associates, 1986)

DECISION MAKING STYLES

STYLE 1
You make the decision yourself and communicate it to the group.

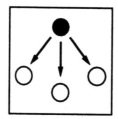

STYLE 2
You gather necessary information from others individually, and then you decide

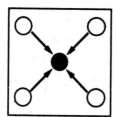

STYLE 3
You share the problem with others individually to get their input and suggestions, and then you decide.

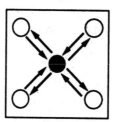

STYLE 4
You share the problem with the group collectively to get their input and suggestions, and then you decide.

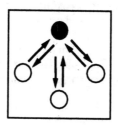

STYLE 5
You share the problem with the group, ask them to come up with a recommended solution, and decide based upon their recommendation.

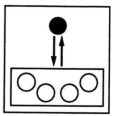

STYLE 6
You share the problem with the group and the group decides with you as an equal member of the group.

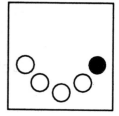

STYLE 7
You share the problem with the group collectively and let the group decide within constraints.

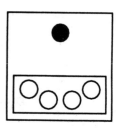

STYLE 8
You delegate the decision to the group and accept their solution.

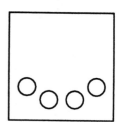

DECISION MAKING FACTORS

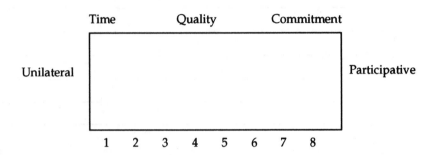

TIME
In general, the more unilateral the style, the less time is required. However, when people have had little involvement in making the decision, more time and effort is usually necessary to motivate them during the implementation phase.

QUALITY
Information: The amount of information you have is likely to affect the quality of the decision.

Some issues benefit from group discussion where various perspectives can come together to define the real problem and consider possible solutions.

Common Goals: When school or team mission and goals have been agreed upon, these can serve as reference points for future decisions and can usually be used to expedite the process.

If the group does not share your or the organization's goals in this area, you are unlikely to want to give up control of the final decision.

COMMITMENT
The more participative the process, the higher the level of acceptance and commitment.

The greater the degree of trust within a team the more willing members are to support each other's decisions without always having to be involved.

There may be some issues — such as those involving confidentiality for either personal, business or legal reasons — that limit the amount of participation possible.

DECISION MAKING WORKSHEET

What is the decision to be made?

_____

_____

_____

_____

_____

_____

Who is involved or will be affected by this decision?

_____

_____

_____

_____

_____

How much time is available for making the decision?

_____

_____

DECISION MAKING WORKSHEET - Continued

QUALITY

		Yes	No	If yes, then consider
1.	Is it true that you do not have enough information yourself to make this decision?	☐	☐	Styles 2, 3, 4, 5, 6, 7, 8
2.	Do you want other's input and suggestions, as well as any information they have?	☐	☐	Styles 3, 4, 5, 6, 7, 8
3.	Are there any benefits to having the group discuss the issue together?	☐	☐	Styles 4, 5, 6, 7, 8

COMMITMENT

1.	Is there likely to be conflict within the group over the best decision which they should work out together?	☐	☐	Styles 5, 6, 7, 8
2.	Is it important that the group be committed to the decision?	☐	☐	Styles 6, 7, 8
3.	Relative to this decision, would it work best if you were perceived as part of the team, rather than as their manager functioning separately from them?	☐	☐	Style 6
4.	Does the group share your goals in this area, and do you trust them to come up with a decision that you can support?	☐	☐	Styles 7, 8
5.	Is this an area for which you want the group to have total ownership, essentially removing yourself from direct involvement?	☐	☐	Style 8

Which decision making styles seem most appropriate in this situation?

   1   2   3   4   5   6   7   8

TEAM PROBLEM SOLVING

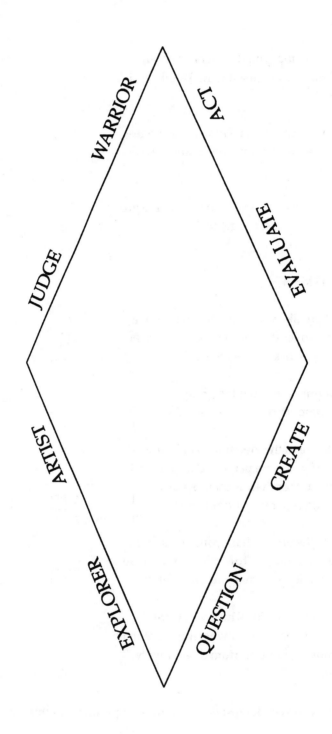

WARRIOR

ACT

JUDGE

EVALUATE

ARTIST

CREATE

EXPLORER

QUESTION

59 So What's the Problem?

A problem well stated is a problem half solved.
—Charles F. Kettering

Introduction

This next series of activities provides a logical sequence for tackling a problem in a collaborative manner.

The first step in the process, **Explorer,*** seeks to define the "real" problem so that any solutions that are implemented actually accomplish what's needed. Often, solutions address the symptoms of a problem rather than the root causes.

Once the problem is defined, the next step, **Artist**, is to put your creative thinking caps on to generate as many potential solutions as possible.

Next, **Judge**, the potential solutions are evaluated in order to determine which one is likely to be most effective in solving the problem.

Finally, **Warrior**, a plan is developed outlining the actions needed to implement the solution.

The process is meant to be highly interactive building group consensus on the problem definition as well as on the final solution. Strong facilitation is critical. Each step in the process must remain distinct, taken in sequence and completed before proceeding with the process.

The group needs to agree that they have accurately defined the problem before moving on to solving it. Likewise, judgment needs to be deferred until after the brainstorming since nothing puts a damper on creative thinking more than having a critic in the group negating some of the suggestions.

---

* The names used to label the four steps of the Problem Solving Process were suggested by Roger von Oech in *A Kick in the Seat of the Pants* (New York: Harper & Row, 1986)

Purpose

The purpose of this exercise is to involve the group in defining clearly what the problem is since how it is defined will determine what the solutions are.

Students being disruptive in class is a problem, but what is the real problem?

- The students are just being mean and ornery?
- The students are suffering from Attention Deficit Disorder?
- Parents are not supporting the schools efforts at disciplining students?
- Teachers are not trained to work with the range of diversity found in today's student populations?
- Class size is inherently unmanageable?
- Teachers are not using teaching strategies that match student learning styles?
- Administrators are not tough enough because they are focusing too much on the student's self-esteem?

Trying to get agreement on what is the real problem may itself turn out to be a real problem. However, to proceed with solutions for student disruptions without a clear sense of what's causing it is likely to result in futile efforts, failed attempts, wasted resources, frustrated staff and . . . disruptive students.

Procedure

1. Identify the problem that needs to be resolved. Select one that is important enough to warrant the investment of time and energy required. The problem should also be one about which this group can actually do something.

2. In order to build commitment to the success of this process, be sure to involve everyone whose support will be required for the solution to work.

3. Estimate how long each of the four steps in the process will take and schedule the meeting or series of meetings to be used for this purpose.

4. Decide on who will facilitate and record each step of the process.

5. The facilitator uses the following guidelines to help the group deepen their understanding of the problem and formulate it in a way that will promote creative solutions.

FACILITATOR GUIDELINES

- Introduce the Session
    Indicate what the current statement of the problem is and explain that the **purpose** of this session is for the group to deepen their understanding of the root causes of the problem — and to reach agreement on a definition of the **real** problem. The **intended result** of the session is to state the problem in terms of a question that will stimulate creative solutions.

- Explore the Problem
    Ask: — What is the problem?
                   — Where is the problem?
                   — When is it a problem?
                   — Whose problem is it?
                   — What makes it a problem?
                   — What do we know?
                   — What don't we know?
                   — What is/is not part of the problem?
                   — What has already been attempted?
                   — Has anyone else dealt with this situation before? What did they discover?
                   — What else do we need to know in order to consider possible solutions?
                   — What factors contribute to this problem?
                   — What are the root causes of this problem?
                   — What is the 'real' problem?

- Transform the Problem into an Opportunity
    State the problem as a question
            — Experiment with a number of different ways of framing the question.
            — Include in the question a measurable objective, if appropriate.

60 The More the Merrier

Imagination was given to man to compensate him for what he is not. A sense of humor was provided to console him for what he is.

—Horace Walpole

Purpose

This is the second step of the Team Problem Solving Process. The purpose is to generate as many solutions as possible to the problem/question being considered.

Procedure

The facilitator uses the following guidelines to conduct this creative brainstorming session.

The recorder writes down every idea on easel pages in view of the entire group.

The group should be facing the wall where the easel pages are posted so that they can see the ideas as they are recorded

FACILITATOR GUIDELINES

- Introduce the Session
  — Indicate that the purpose of this session is to brainstorm as many potential solutions as possible. Invite the group to be playful, wild and crazy, and to avoid editing their thoughts or judging any ideas.
  — Write the problem/question on a chart and post it so that everyone can see it.
  — Start by stating the agreed-upon problem/question. (Refer back to the problem/question throughout the process.)

- Brainstorm Alternatives
  — Review guidelines for brainstorming:
    √   Everyone contributes as many ideas as possible.
    √   Okay to piggy-back on other's ideas.
    √   Avoid discussing ideas at this point.
    √   Defer judgment until next phase.

- Establish an Objective and Time Limit
  — "Let's see if we can generate twenty ideas in the next ten minutes."

- Stimulate Creativity
  — If the ideas begin to wane, invite the group to look at the problem/question from different perspectives.
    √   "If you were the students, what would the solution look like?"
    √   "If you were in charge, how would you solve it?"
    √   "If you were an outside consultant known for innovative solutions, what would you recommend?"
    √   "If you were from another planet that had solved the problem, what solution was used?"

- Include Everyone
  — If some people have not offered any ideas, draw them out and invite them to contribute.

- Summarize
  — Before moving on to the next phase, restate the problem/question and acknowledge the group's creativity in generating all these possible solutions.

61 Here Comes the Judge

Nothing is more dangerous than an idea when it is the only one you have.

—Emile Chartier

Purpose

As the third step in the Team Problem Solving sequence, this activity is intended to have the group come to consensus on the best solution to the problem/question being considered.

Procedure

The facilitator uses these guidelines to evaluate the list of possible solutions and move the group to agreeing on which will work best.

FACILITATOR GUIDELINES

- **Introduce the Session**
  - Refer to the easel pages of ideas that were generated during the brainstorming and indicate that the purpose of this session is to evaluate these potential solutions in order to select the one that is likely to be most effective. The intended result is the group arriving at a consensus as to the best course of action.

- **Adopt Group Wisdom**
  - Invite the group to accept a sense of team ownership for all the ideas that were generated and let go of attaching personal ownership for a particular idea. This will make it easier to evaluate the solutions objectively without individuals trying to protect and defend their own ideas.

- **Refine the List**
  - Before proceeding, ask the group if some of the items can be combined, clustered, or eliminated in order to simplify the list, reduce the total number and make it more manageable.

- **Establish Criteria**
  - Consider what criteria would need to be met in order for a solution to be workable. Do this before evaluating any of the alternatives.
  - Brainstorm possible criteria. Agree on criteria that are essential. Prioritize the list of criteria.

- **Evaluate the Alternatives**
  - The criteria can be used in a structured process by drawing a matrix with the alternative solutions down one side and the criteria across the top. Each solution is measured against the criteria to determine whether it meets the criteria (on a numerical scale). This process can be time consuming. You may want to use one of the following strategies to limit the alternatives first.
  - Reduce the total number of alternative solutions.
    - √ Divide the total number of items on the list by three and let each team member select that many items to keep on the list for further consideration. For example, if the total number of items is 21, everyone gets to choose the 7 alternatives that they feel are most promising. After everyone has indicated their choices, the items selected most often remain on the list and the others are eliminated.
    - √ An alternative method, is to let everyone pick their top 3 choices. This could also be weighted so that first choice gets 3 points, second 2, third choice 1. Those items receiving the most points remain on the list.
    - √ Another approach is to start by asking which items on the list can be eliminated because they are clearly too outrageous, not practical or do not meet any of the criteria. One of the strategies mentioned above can then be used to reduce the list further.

- Begin to seek consensus
    - When the list of alternative solutions to the problem/question has been reduced to a few best possibilities, have the group compare and contrast the remaining options toward selecting one of these to implement.
        - √ Do a structured criteria matrix analysis (described earlier).
        - √ Identify advantages and disadvantages of each.
        - √ Go around the group and have each team member talk about which one they like best and what they like about it.
        - √ If most of the group is leaning toward one of the solutions and a few team members are not yet sold on the idea, have them address what concerns them about it. Explore whether the solution can be modified to address these concerns. See if there is a way of combining a couple of solutions so that the final outcome accommodates everyone's needs.
    - Be persistent about a win/win solution.

- What to do if . . .
    - If the group is unable to come to consensus on the best solution to the problem, you can
        - √ Schedule a follow-up session when the group will reconvene to decide on the matter at that time. Discuss what could happen in the meantime to help bring the group to consensus (e.g. more research could be done, other's opinions could be sought, people with concerns could return with a modified solution that would work for them).
        - √ Summarize the findings of this group including unresolved issues that blocked consensus and refer the final decision to the appropriate person in the organization.
        - √ By consensus, the group could agree to allow the decision to be made by majority rule and then, let the group vote.

62 Just Do It

People who say it cannot be done should not interrupt those who are doing it.

—Author Unknown

Purpose

This is the final stage of the Team Problem Solving Process. Now that a solution has been identified, the purpose of this exercise is to develop a plan for implementing that solution.

Procedure

The facilitator uses the following guidelines to help the group develop its action plan.

FACILITATOR GUIDELINES

- Introduce the Session
    - Now that a solution has been identified, the purpose of this meeting is for us to develop a plan of action. The intended result is for us to have a written plan including what actions need to be taken, who will be responsible for each action and what our timeline is for the plan.

- Develop an Implementation Plan
    - Make a chart with columns headed WHAT, WHO and WHEN.
    - Brainstorm all the action steps that need to be done in order to implement the plan from beginning to end. (An alternative to the chart is to record each activity on a separate index card and then move the cards around until a logical sequence of events has been established. This can then be drawn into a flow chart.)
    - For each action item, have a group member sign up to be responsible for accomplishing it.
    - Ask the person who is responsible for completing the item what their time frame is.

- Include a Feedback Mechanism
    - Ongoing evaluation will allow for modifying the plan during implementation.
    - A final assessment will provide a sense of closure and serve as an opportunity to acknowledge success.

- Arrange to have copies of the plan distributed so that everyone has a record of their individual commitments as well as the group's overall game plan.

Chapter 8

Conflict Management

The moral absolute should be: if and when, in any dispute, one side initiates the use of physical force, that side is wrong — and no consideration or discussion of the issues is necessary or appropriate.

—Ayn Rand

Chapter 8   Conflict Management

Problems are only opportunities in work clothes.

—Henry J. Kaiser

Introduction

If a team does not experience tension, disagreement and conflict, it is probably not being very productive.

Differences of opinion are bound to exist; that is part of the purpose of using a team approach to accomplishing a project. If everyone feels exactly the same way about everything, then there is too much redundancy on the team or people are lying.

If the second is true, then the team is stuck at the Forming Stage of team building and will not evolve to a high performing team unless an environment is created that makes it safe for people to disagree and use this energy to arrive at innovative solutions in a collaborative manner.

There are three approaches to managing conflict. The first is **proactive**: creating the conditions that allow conflict to be perceived by the team as a healthy part of the process. Being proactive includes establishing ground rules and protocol for how conflict will be used in a productive way. Much of the material in this chapter can be used for this purpose. Specifically: Team Communication (Activity 41); Team Trust (Activity 42); Learning from the Past (Activity 44); Stormy Weather (Activity 45); Team Balance (Activity 46); Team Agreements (Activity 49).

A second approach to conflict could be called **interactive** in that it deals with the situations as they arise to extract the benefits of the differing points of view while averting the negative feelings that could result if the issue escalated to an actual conflict.

If the proactive and interactive methods are not applied or do not work to de-escalate the conflict before a full-blown confrontation occurs, then the **retroactive** approach can be used.

63 Interactive Interventions

People who fight fire with fire usually end up with ashes.
—Abigail Van Buren

Purpose

In your role as leader/facilitator you will have opportunities to intervene as differences of opinion arise among team members to redirect the energy into a positive direction — to "transform the storming" if you will.

It is difficult to predict in the abstract which of these techniques will work best given the situation and the people involved. The diagnostic tools should provide you with at least some guidance.

Procedure

When tension begins to develop among team members and you are concerned it might escalate to conflict or confrontation, select one of the intervention techniques that seems appropriate to the situation.

DIAGNOSTIC TOOL	INTERVENTION TECHNIQUE
If a couple of team members are arguing back and forth without listening to the other person's point:	Then ask them to restate the other person's point of view before repeating their own.
If one person is blaming someone else for something:	Then ask how he or she may have contributed to the problem.
If a couple of people are arguing over the facts of what happened:	Then ask them to distinguish between the actual event and how they interpreted the event.
If someone is building a case by over-generalizing:	Then ask him or her to be more specific and precise in recounting the events.
If someone constantly refers back to some past wrong doing:	Then acknowledge that what happened, happened and we can not go back and make it happen differently. Then ask them to state their specific request for how they would like something like this handled in the future.
If the team seems to be bogged down in the negative aspects of a problem:	Then reframe the discussion by asking in what way is this problem an opportunity for the team.
If someone is obviously emotional, feeling upset or hurt:	Then give them a chance to express their feelings without anyone interrupting, rebutting or being judgmental.
If someone seems insistent on proving themselves to be right:	Then acknowledge they have a valid point and then ask if they are more committed to being right or resolving the issue.
If people have become stuck in their own point of view and seem unable to understand the other perspective:	Then ask them to pretend to adopt the opposing point of view and to argue that point as vigorously as possible.
If the argument starts to sound like personal attack:	Then ask those involved to not deliver it nor take it personally — to attack the problem not the person.
If the disagreement seems to be around how to accomplish something (methods and procedures):	Then focus those involved on the purpose of doing it, and seek common ground at this level.

If the conflict involves differences in beliefs and values:	Then ask the conflictees to seek a deeper understanding of the other person's context, to put the disputed belief and value in this person's context not your own, and to accept the other's context as one way of relating to the world.
If the dispute seems to exist in a WIN/LOSE context — all solutions involve one side winning at the other's expense:	Then establish the best long-term solution for the team has got to be one where both sides get their needs met. Ask those involved to adopt a WIN/WIN context and to brainstorm solutions in a spirit of true collaboration.
If the discussion of the issue has been extensive and all the talking has not yielded a positive result:	Then ask everyone to be silent for awhile, to go within themselves to a more peaceful place, a place of deeper or higher wisdom, and to pray for, meditate on or contemplate a successful resolution.
	You may want to keep everyone in the room or take a short break, or end the meeting and ask people to "sleep on it."
	When the group reconvenes, go around and ask each person to contribute an idea in support of resolving this issue.

64 Retroactive Resolutions

Truth arises from disagreement amongst friends.

—David Hume

Purpose

This activity takes a collaborative problem-solving approach to resolving conflict. Unlike compromise which is the best that can be expected in a WIN/LOSE context — both sides gain a little and both sides give up a little — true collaboration requires a commitment to a WIN/WIN solution.

Procedure

These seven steps can be used by those involved in the conflict or a facilitator may guide the conflictees through the process.

1. **Create the Context of Collaboration**
   Reiterate that the purpose of this process is to resolve the conflict so that we can continue to be productive.

   In order to accomplish this, both of us need to act with a real concern for each other's needs and feelings, and we need to be committed to creating a solution that works for both of us.

2. **One person expresses his or her position** calmly with the intention of being understood.

   The other listens actively — without becoming emotional, defensive or judgmental — intending to understand the other's point of view.

   The listener restates what he or she understood from what the other said.

   The speaker confirms what was accurately heard and clarifies any misunderstanding.

3. **The second person expresses his or her position** and the process continues in the same manner as step 2.

4. **Create a joint statement of the problem**.
Both parties work together to determine the nature of the conflict and agree on a final statement of the problem as being accurate in addressing both their needs.

5. **Brainstorm possible solutions**.
Working together once again in collaboration, the two individuals generate as many creative alternatives as possible.

Standard rules for brainstorm — defer judgment and so forth — are in effect.

6. **Agree on a solution**.
Review the list and begin to narrow down the options. Discuss the pros and cons of the ones that seem most workable. The process is not over until consensus is achieved. If one person's preferred solution does not work for the other person then it doesn't work.

The final solution is one with which both parties can live.

7. **Develop an action plan**.
In order to ensure that the agreed-upon solution is carried out, decide what needs to be done by whom and when.

If appropriate, report back to the full team that the conflict has been resolved.

Part IV

Leadership of Organizations:
Facilitating Change

An organization of leaders, all sharing the same vision and purpose, can be a powerful force. But for that new organization to work, everyone in it must be given real work to do, work that focuses on making the vision and purpose real...

—James Champy

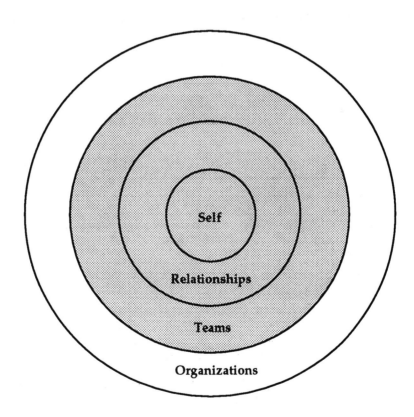

Part Four   Leadership of Organizations: Facilitating Change

Corporations and government must be transformed, and so must we. The race will go to the curious, the slightly mad, and those with an unsated passion for learning and daredeviltry.
—Tom Peters

Introduction

Organizational transformation is really a chicken-and-egg type situation. An organization changes as a result of individuals within it leading the change. On the other hand, individuals can only change to the degree that the organization provides an environment that supports it.

As in relationships, when one partner grows faster than or in different directions from the other, a split-up is almost inevitable. So too, in organizations, if you want to keep your best people you must create a culture that is dynamic, challenging, that rewards risk and celebrates innovation.

Chapter 9

Strategic Planning

*L*eaders require foresight, so that they can judge how the vision fits into the way the environment of the organization may evolve; hindsight, so that the vision does not violate the traditions and culture of the organization; a worldview, within which to interpret the impact of possible new developments and trends; depth perception, so that the possible responses of competitors and other stakeholders to the new direction can be comprehended; and a process of revision, so that all visions previously synthesized are constantly reviewed as the environment changes.

—Warren Bennis and Burt Nanus

Chapter 9   Strategic Planning

You must not change one thing, one pebble, one grain of sand, until you know what good and evil will follow on the act.
—Ursula K. LeGuin

Introduction

The purpose of Strategic Planning is to create a blueprint for the future. While it is impossible to predict exactly what the world will look like five years from now, having a plan for where your organization wants to be will greatly increase the likelihood of that goal being achieved.

The planning process itself is invaluable as a team building experience. All the various constituents need to discuss a variety of critical issues, explore a diversity of opinions and seek consensus on priorities.

This chapter provides activities corresponding to each of the components of a Strategic Plan.

65 Plan to Plan

*P*lan your work and work your plan.

—Anonymous

Purpose

The first thing to consider when embarking on a strategic planning process is who needs to be involved and at what level.

The key here is to strike a balance between two opposing facts:

- the more involved people are in the process, the more ownership and commitment they feel to its success;

- the more people who are involved, the more difficult it is to agree on anything, and the longer the process takes.

Procedure

1. Bring together the appropriate group of decision makers. (For example, School-Site Council, School Management Team or Full Staff; District Management Team, Superintendent's Council or Board of Education.)

2. Using a chart similar to the one on the Plan to Plan Worksheet, decide who is to be involved in developing the plan directly and who will be involved in a more indirect manner. Across the top of the chart write in the names of individuals and groups who are to be included.

   In the left hand column fill in the steps in the process that are to be completed.

   In the boxes corresponding to the top and side columns indicate D for direct involvement and I for indirect.

   Examples of direct involvement include:

   - deciding what is actually included in final plan

- recommending what ought to be included in sections of the plan
- participating in planning meetings and brainstorming sessions.

Indirect involvement might include:

- helping facilitate the process
- serving on a panel of experts
- participating in focus groups offering opinions on certain topics
- responding in writing to a survey soliciting input.

3. From this analysis, establish a Core Planning Team who will coordinate the overall process.

PLAN TO PLAN WORKSHEET

CONSTITUENTS / STAKEHOLDERS

STEPS IN THE PLANNING PROCESS	Board of Education	Superintendent	District Administrators	Principal	Site Administrator	Teachers	Students	Parents	Community	Experts/Consultants
Current Profile										
Environmental Scan										
Purpose/Mission/Vision										
Goals/Objectives										
Strategies/Actions										
Performance Assessment										

66 Conducting a Values Audit

If you are planning for one year, grow rice.
If you are planning for 20 years, grow trees.
If you are planning for centuries, grow men.

—Chinese proverb

Purpose

Having determined who is to be involved in the Strategic Planning Process, the next logical step is to do an assessment of your organization's — school or district — current situation. Knowing where you are today is essential to being able to plan where you intend to be in the future.

A good place to start with the current profile is a Values Audit. This is an articulation of principles and beliefs that guide the organization's behavior. Gaps between stated beliefs and actual practices are revealed as part of the audit.

Procedure

1. Bring together the team designated to conduct the Values Audit.

2. Distribute copies of the Values Audit Worksheet and ask each person to complete the form.

3. Ask the team to inform you of any value they rated a 5 (most important) and record these on easel pad pages or large sheets of butcher paper so that they are visible to the group.

   If the same value is mentioned by more than one person, add a check mark next to it rather than writing it again.

4. Add up the check marks and number the values in terms of most frequently mentioned.

   Allow time for discussion.

5. Now have each team member read out the Current Performance rating they gave to the most frequently mentioned values.

Add up the scores and divide by the number of responses to get an average rating. Call attention to those values that received consistently high scores by putting a ★ (star) next to them. Put a ▲ (delta) symbol next to those items receiving consistently low scores. Put a ? (question mark) next to those whose scores were widely spread.

Invite discussion at this point.

Questions to explore include:

- Who should be acknowledged for the areas receiving high scores?

- How do we explain the variation in scores on those items with a wide spread?

- What do we need to do to behave more consistently with those values rated as important but receiving low scores in terms of current performance?

VALUES AUDIT WORKSHEET

Start with the values listed and add any additional values you feel are essential, or use a completely blank worksheet. Rate each one in terms of importance on a scale from 1 (least important) to 5 (most important). Also indicate how well you think the school is currently performing relative to each of the values on a 1 (very poor) to 5 (very good).

VALUES	IMPORTANCE	CURRENT PERFORMANCE
• Visionary leadership	_____	_____
• Clear and focused mission	_____	_____
• Accountability for student performance	_____	_____
• Collaboration and empowerment	_____	_____
• Site-based decision making	_____	_____
• Parent and community involvement	_____	_____
• Expanded use of technology	_____	_____
• Other		
_____	_____	_____
_____	_____	_____
_____	_____	_____
_____	_____	_____
_____	_____	_____
_____	_____	_____
_____	_____	_____
_____	_____	_____
_____	_____	_____
_____	_____	_____

67 Current Profile

The real problems confronting schools are enormous in comparison with any ideal situations. The gap between what is known and what is in practice is enormous in nearly every school setting.

—Ben Harris

Purpose

In addition to the Values Audit, other aspects of the Internal Analysis might include:

- Scope of current services or programs
- Common characteristics of services or programs
- User groups/clients served by the services or programs
- Assessment of effectiveness of services or programs including client satisfaction measures and a cost/benefit analysis
- Current strengths/areas of excellence
- Current weaknesses/areas for improvement

Procedure

1. Have the Core Planning Team meet to scope out the range of services or programs offered by the department, school or district, and to identify what the programs have in common.

2. The Core Team plans the most effective means of gathering the rest of the data for the Current Profile. Delegating the task to people within each program works well provided the organizational climate allows for honest feedback rather than political posturing.

3. Distribute copies of the Current Profile Packet to those charged with gathering this information.

4. Core Team meets to review the reports from each program, and to compile a composite Profile for the organization.

CURRENT PROFILE PACKET

Name of Program _____

User Groups/Clients Served
(Who receives benefit from this program and how many people are served?)

_____

_____

_____

_____

_____

CURRENT PROFILE

CLIENT SATISFACTION SURVEY

What aspects of this program are most important to you?

How well is the program meeting your needs? *

_____   _____

_____   _____

_____   _____

_____   _____

_____   _____

_____   _____

* Scale

1	2	3	4
Very Unsatisfactory	Somewhat Satisfactory	Moderately Satisfactory	Very Satisfactory

What aspects of the program are working best for you?

_____

_____

_____

What aspects of the program are in need of the greatest improvement?

_____

_____

_____

CURRENT PROFILE

COST/BENEFIT ANALYSIS

Who is benefiting from this program?

What benefits are our user groups/clients receiving from this program?

What benefits are we (staff, school, district, and so forth) receiving from this program?

How much does this program cost? What is the cost per student or cost per client served?

Is it worth it?

CURRENT PROFILE

STRENGTHS/WEAKNESSES

What are the strengths of this program? What's working?

What areas need to be improved? What's not working?

68 Environmental Scan (External Analysis)

Everything is more complicated than it seems.

—Murphy's Law

Purpose

All organizations exist in a larger environment that includes the community, political pressures, social concerns, economic realities and so forth. In order to plan for a successful future, it is helpful to consider external factors likely to have an impact on the organization's ability to achieve its mission.

The environmental scan is often done in terms of:

- Opportunities — conditions and trends that could prove advantageous

- Threats — facts that could prove detrimental to the organization's future success

Procedure

1. The Core Planning Team may be sufficiently familiar with current trends to be able to conduct this analysis. However, it may prove helpful to hear from experts who could speak to issues likely to affect the school or district.

2. Brainstorm a list of possible experts who could speak to the Core Team on future trends. Such experts might include:
   - educational leaders
   - former students
   - business leaders
   - community leaders
   - political activists/government officials
   - economists
   - consultants, authors who have written on related topics
   - representatives from other schools or districts who have gone through a similar process.

3. Schedule meetings with these experts to gather information toward creating a picture of probable futures.

4. In preparation for these meetings, have the Core Team consider the following three realms of knowledge.

- **What we know we know** about the future, and what questions can we ask to validate our knowledge?

- **What do we know we don't know** about the future and what questions do we have that we would like answered?

- **What don't we know we don't know** and how can we stay open to discovering the questions we need to be asking?

69 Purpose Statement

The object of purposing is the stirring of human consciousness, the enhancement of meaning, the spelling out of key cultural strands that provides both excitement and significance to one's work.

—Thomas Sergiovanni

Purpose

As discussed in Part I of this book (Activity 1), a purpose statement describes the most fundamental reason for which something exists.

The purpose statement is the foundation upon which the mission, vision and goals are based.

Procedure

1. Members of the group identified as directly involved in defining the Purpose/Mission of the school/district or organization are asked to state what they feel is the purpose.

2. This group is asked to reflect on the purpose from various viewpoints:
   - What is society's purpose?
   - What is the immediate community's purpose?
   - What purpose do people in business think is important?
   - What is the purpose from the parent's viewpoint?
   - What do students think is the purpose?

3. These various statements of purpose are discussed and common themes are explored.

4. Select a few of the purpose statements for further consideration. With each one ask "What is the purpose of that?" Continue asking this same question until it seems that there is no where else to go and a bottom line purpose statement has been reached.

For example:

"The purpose of education is to teach students how to learn."

"What is the purpose of that?"

"So that they can acquire knowledge and develop skills."

"What is the purpose of that?"

"So that they can pursue a career they will enjoy."

"What is the purpose of that?"

"So they will be successful."

"What is the purpose of that?"

"So that they can be financially secure and provide for themselves and their families."

"What is the purpose of that?"

"So that they can feel productive, loved and happy."

"What is the purpose of that?"

"That's it. That's all there is."

So, in this example, the purpose of education is to provide students with the knowledge and skills they need to be successful so that they can feel productive, loved and happy.

Or, more succinctly, the purpose of education is to create loving, happy and productive people.

70 Mission Statement

Give the mission charisma and staying power. If a mission is to compel the actions of all staff, it must be attractive, meaningful, and highly influential.

—Kathryn S. Whitaker and Monte C. Moses

Purpose

The Mission Statement defines what function the organization performs or what is its business.

The Mission Statement comes out of the purpose, and states what the organization contributes to whom, with what intended result.

Procedure

1. Hand out copies of the Organizational Mission Worksheet to the team responsible for the Purpose/Mission component of the Strategic Plan.

2. Have each person fill out the sheet first.

3. Starting with the first question, have the team members read what they wrote, and discuss the various ideas. Work toward achieving consensus on what the school's mission is.

4. Use the same process on question two until the team agrees on to whom the school is looking to contribute.

5. Once again, explore question three regarding the scope or intended result of the contribution, facilitating the discussion in support of team alignment.

6. Finally, combine the answers to the three questions to form one Mission Statement.

ORGANIZATIONAL MISSION WORKSHEET

1. What do we as an educational institution contribute?

   _____

   _____

   _____

2. To whom do we contribute? Who are the benefactors?

   _____

   _____

   _____

3. Toward what end is our contribution aimed? What positive outcomes occur as a result of our contribution?

   _____

   _____

   _____

ORGANIZATIONAL MISSION STATEMENT

Now combine your answer to the three questions into one statement.

_____

_____

_____

_____

71 Strategic Vision

*V*ision animates, inspirits, transforms purpose into action.
—Warren Bennis and Burt Nanus

Purpose

This superordinate goal defines a long-range target that both inspires the imagination and establishes a direction on which practical decisions can be based. As mentioned in Activity 3, "Putting a man on the moon by the end of the decade" — a vision articulated by President Kennedy in 1960 — is an excellent example.

Unlike the Purpose and Mission Statements, which are ongoing in nature, a Vision Statement is an end point.

Procedure

1. Review the guidelines for creative brainstorming.

2. Ask the question:
   "Given our purpose and mission, what is the greatest we could imagine accomplishing within the next five years?"

3. Record all the ideas on easel pages or large pieces of butcher paper posted where everyone can see.

   Encourage the team to think big, reach high, to go for greatness.

4. After the brainstorming, the group discusses the alternatives and agrees on a Vision. The facilitator guidelines outlined in Innovative Problem Solving, Here Comes the Judge (Activity 61) can be used here.

72 GOALS — Long-Range

> **G**o as far as you can see,
> and when you get there,
> you will see farther.
>
> —Anonymous

Purpose

Now that the Strategic Vision has been established, goals can be set to spell out the major milestones between now and the realization of the vision.

The goals are to be identified for key areas and be placed in a time frame such as:
- Long-range (3-5 years)
- Intermediate (2-3 years)
- Short-term (1-2 years).

Procedure

1. Ask the Planning Team to respond to the question:
   "In order for us to realize our Strategic Vision, what goals will we need to have achieved?"

   Record the answers on easel pages or butcher paper.

2. Continue to stimulate people's thinking by asking some follow-up questions such as:
   "What goals do we want to have achieved in the areas of:
   - student achievement?
   - full inclusion?
   - parent involvement?
   - technology?
   - staff development?
   - fundraising?"

3. Review the Values Audit for areas to improve that ought to be set as goals, and add these to this list.

4. When the Current Profile (Internal Analysis) is completed, review programmatic areas to improve for possible inclusion.

5. When the Environmental Scan (External Analysis) is completed, review the Opportunities section for suggestions to include as goals and consider the potential threats for indications of goals to overcome these obstacles.

6. Develop a criteria for selecting which goals from this expansive list to include as part of the Strategic Plan.

   Possible criteria might include:
   - It's essential to our purpose, mission and vision
   - Is it demanded by our clients
   - It builds upon our strengths
   - It is a serious weakness that must be addressed
   - It can realistically be accomplished
   - The resources exist or can be acquired to achieve it.

7. Review all the possible goals in light of the criteria and select the ones to include. Inclusion in the plan ought to be viewed as a commitment to realizing them.

73 GOALS — Intermediate and Short-Term

If you chase two rabbits, both will escape.

—Anonymous

Purpose

Long-range goals are important in defining the direction you are headed. They remain dreams until they are translated into intermediate and short-term goals.

Procedure

1. The goals that are to be achieved at the program level ought to be communicated to the people who will be responsible for achieving them. They can set the intermediate and short-term goals for their areas.

2. Hand out copies of the Goals Worksheet with the long-range goals listed.

3. Identify intermediate and short-term goals for each of the long-range goals.

GOALS WORKSHEET

LONG-RANGE GOALS (3-5 years)	INTERMEDIATE GOALS (2-3 years)	SHORT-TERM GOALS (1-2 years)
1. _____ _____ _____ _____	1. _____ _____ _____ _____	1. _____ _____ _____ _____
2. _____ _____ _____ _____	2. _____ _____ _____ _____	2. _____ _____ _____ _____
3. _____ _____ _____ _____	3. _____ _____ _____ _____	3. _____ _____ _____ _____
4. _____ _____ _____ _____	4. _____ _____ _____ _____	4. _____ _____ _____ _____
5. _____ _____ _____ _____	5. _____ _____ _____ _____	5. _____ _____ _____ _____

74 Objectives

Institutions mistake good intentions for objectives. They say "health care;" that's an intention, not an objective.

—Peter Drucker

Purpose

Objectives are measurable. Translating a goal into an objective requires a rigorous process of determining how the results will be quantified.

It's a common organizational philosophy: "If you can't measure it, you can't manage it."

Procedure

1. Hand out copies of the Objectives Worksheet with the short-term goals listed.

2. Have the group identify objectives for each goal and how these will be measured. Each goal may have more than one objective. The objectives ought to answer how much, how many, to what degree, what percentage, and so forth. The measures ought to explain how you will know the objective is achieved, i.e. test scores, numbers of students, survey results, and so forth.

3. Again, objectives and measures for program goals ought to be established by those responsible for achieving them.

OBJECTIVES WORKSHEET

SHORT-TERM GOALS (1-2 years)	OBJECTIVES	MEASURES
1. _____ _____ _____ _____	1.1 _____ _____ _____ _____	_____ _____ _____ _____
	1.2 _____ _____ _____ _____	_____ _____ _____ _____
	1.3 _____ _____ _____ _____	_____ _____ _____ _____
2. _____ _____ _____ _____	2.1 _____ _____ _____ _____	_____ _____ _____ _____
	2.2 _____ _____ _____ _____	_____ _____ _____ _____
	2.3 _____ _____ _____ _____	_____ _____ _____ _____

SHORT-TERM GOALS (1-2 years)	OBJECTIVES	MEASURES
3. _____ _____ _____ _____	3.1 _____ _____ _____ _____	_____ _____ _____ _____
	3.2 _____ _____ _____ _____	_____ _____ _____ _____
	3.3 _____ _____ _____ _____	_____ _____ _____ _____
4. _____ _____ _____ _____	4.1 _____ _____ _____ _____	_____ _____ _____ _____
	4.2 _____ _____ _____ _____	_____ _____ _____ _____
	4.3 _____ _____ _____ _____	_____ _____ _____ _____

SHORT-TERM GOALS (1-2 years)	OBJECTIVES	MEASURES
5. _____ _____ _____ _____	5.1 _____ _____ _____ _____	_____ _____ _____ _____
	5.2 _____ _____ _____ _____	_____ _____ _____ _____
	5.3 _____ _____ _____ _____	_____ _____ _____ _____

75 Strategies

All men can see these tactics whereby I conquer, but what none can see is the strategy out of which victory is evolved.

—Sun-tzu

Purpose

For every major objective, strategies need to be developed which address how the objectives are to be met, through what means or sustained course of action.

Procedure

1. Hand out the Strategies Worksheet with the objectives identified.

2. For each objective, identify strategies to be used.

3. Strategies for program objectives should be set at that level.

STRATEGIES WORKSHEET

OBJECTIVES	STRATEGIES

1.1 _____   _____
    _____   _____
    _____   _____

1.2 _____   _____
    _____   _____
    _____   _____

1.3 _____   _____
    _____   _____
    _____   _____

2.1 _____   _____
    _____   _____
    _____   _____

2.2 _____   _____
    _____   _____
    _____   _____

2.3 _____   _____
    _____   _____
    _____   _____

76 Action Plans

It's not the same to talk of bulls, as to be in the bullring.
—Spanish Proverb

Purpose

The strategies identified in the previous activity now need to be turned into an action plan detailing step-by-step who does what by when.

Procedure

1. Action plans are best developed by the people who will be responsible for carrying them out.

2. Hand out copies of the Action Plan Worksheet to the groups involved.

3. Completed copies of the forms, along with forms distributed for the previous activities need to be returned to the Core Planning Team for inclusion in the Strategic Planning document.

ACTION PLANS WORKSHEET

GOAL 1   _____

                      _____

                      _____

OBJECTIVE 1.1 _____

                      _____

                      _____

STRATEGY   _____

                      _____

                      _____

ACTION PLAN

WHAT	WHO	WHEN
_____	_____	_____
_____	_____	_____
_____	_____	_____
_____	_____	_____
_____	_____	_____
_____	_____	_____
_____	_____	_____
_____	_____	_____
_____	_____	_____
_____	_____	_____
_____	_____	_____
_____	_____	_____
_____	_____	_____
_____	_____	_____
_____	_____	_____

Chapter 10

Managing the Change Process

> *T*he only person who likes change is a wet baby.
>
> —Roy Blitzer

Chapter 10 Managing the Change Process

To blind oneself to change is not therefore to halt it.

—Isaac Goldberg

Introduction

Developing a Strategic Plan is often difficult enough. Implementing the plan in order to produce substantive change is the real test of your leadership skills.

The purpose of this chapter is to help you navigate through the often turbulent and sometimes treacherous waters of change.

Attempting change without a comprehensive plan for aligning all the organizational dimensions of the school environment will produce anxiety, cynicism, false starts and spotty results as shown in the chart below.

LEADERSHIP FOR CHANGE

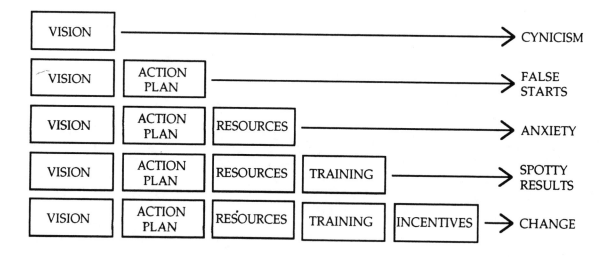

Having a Philosophy, Purpose, Mission and Vision is essential to change. However, if there is no follow-through or real support, people become cynical and disillusioned.

As indicated in the previous chapter on Strategic Planning, translating the Vision into Goals, Objectives and Action Plans is critical in making the change process real. Once again, without the necessary resources, training and incentives, just having a plan will likely lead to a series of false starts that are not sustained over time.

Adequate training is required in order for the people who are expected to make changes to get beyond their anxiety and become competent and confident in their ability to perform in new ways.

Finally, the incentives, rewards and recognition need to be aligned with the desired change. If, for example, the school wants to change to a form of "authentic assessment" such as portfolios, and yet the teachers' effectiveness is measured by standardized test scores, then most teachers will continue to focus on the standardized measures. Only those who are passionately dedicated to the change will persevere, and the results will be spotty, at best.

77 Now and Then

It is the business of the future to be dangerous.
—Alfred North Whitehead

Purpose

The Visioning exercise done as part of the Strategic Planning is often idealistic, abstract and hypothetical. The point of this activity is to establish a sharp contrast between the vision and the current situation so that everyone involved has a clear sense of the changes to be anticipated.

Procedure

1. Schedule a staff meeting to discuss the changes implied in the school's Strategic Plan.

2. On easel pads or butcher paper create two columns headed "Now" and "Then."

3. Ask staff members to refer to the Vision and Goals sections of the Strategic Plan to find something that will change about the school as the plan is implemented. Record the change in the "Then" column. Then ask the group to indicate how things are now relative to this area. Record their comments in the "Now" column.

4. Continue the process until all the major changes have been mentioned and compared with how things are at the moment.

5. End with an opportunity for each staff person to comment on how he or she feels about the intended changes: What's exciting? What's frightening?, and so forth.

78 Who Me?

An Eastern European economist was discussing the economy of his country with a Western journalist. He said, "There are only two ways to restore and revive the economy — the natural way or the miraculous way."

"The natural or miraculous way?" the journalist questioned.

"Yes. The natural way would be if a group of angels came down from heaven and created jobs and prosperity for everyone."

"That's the natural way?" the journalist blurted, "Then what's the miraculous way?"

"If we took the initiative and did it ourselves," he retorted.

—Author Unknown

Purpose

The Goals, Objectives and Actions contained in the Strategic Plan are likely to have been developed from a school-wide perspective. Now it is time for each individual staff person to confront his or her own responsibility for implementing the plan.

Procedure

1. Reconvene the staff for another meeting and have the "Now and Then" (Activity 77) sheets posted.

2. Have staff members read through the "Now and Then" lists, and complete the "Who Me" Worksheet by writing down the items that affect them directly and indirectly.

WHO ME? WORKSHEET

Review the list from the "Now and Then" sheets. Please record which of the changes will involve you directly and which ones will involve you only indirectly.

DIRECT INVOLVEMENT   INDIRECT INVOLVEMENT

_____   _____
_____   _____
_____   _____
_____   _____
_____   _____
_____   _____
_____   _____
_____   _____
_____   _____
_____   _____
_____   _____
_____   _____
_____   _____
_____   _____
_____   _____
_____   _____
_____   _____
_____   _____
_____   _____
_____   _____
_____   _____
_____   _____

WHO ME? WORKSHEET

Page 2

In order to develop your own Action Plan, select the change area to focus on first because it is the most immediate, most important or most logically precedes the others. Think through all of the individual tasks involved, number them by sequence and create a timeline.

ACTION PLAN

TASK	SEQUENCE	DATE
_____	____	_____
_____	____	_____
_____	____	_____
_____	____	_____
_____	____	_____
_____	____	_____
_____	____	_____
_____	____	_____
_____	____	_____
_____	____	_____
_____	____	_____
_____	____	_____
_____	____	_____
_____	____	_____
_____	____	_____
_____	____	_____
_____	____	_____
_____	____	_____
_____	____	_____
_____	____	_____

79 HELP

When one is helping another, both are strong.

—German Proverb

Purpose

Many attempts at educational innovation fail due to lack of resources.

This activity asks individual staff members to identify what resources they will require, and then, as a group, to create a list of their collective needs.

Procedure

1. Hand out copies of the HELP Worksheet, and ask staff members to identify what resources they will require to carry out their Action Plan (Who Me?, Activity 78).

2. Invite the staff to meet as a group and to bring their HELP Worksheets with them.

3. Go around the group and have each person read his or her list of INTERNAL RESOURCES.

4. Next, do a second round on EXTERNAL RESOURCES, this time recording them on easel pages. Record all the EXTERNAL RESOURCES required by the first person. With each subsequent person put a check mark next to any resource already mentioned and add any new items.

5. Label the list of EXTERNAL RESOURCES "RESOURCES REQUIRED." Now, put the heading "RESOURCES AVAILABLE" on the top of another easel page and ask the group to brainstorm resources that are available to them. This might include: fellow staff members sharing expertise, staff at other school sites who have already been trained, consultants from the State Department of Education, local colleges and universities, grants from Foundations, support from local business and so forth.

6. Suggest that project teams be formed where people with common needs work together to acquire the necessary resources.

7. Check if there is any Resource Required and not available that is so crucial to the success of the program as to suggest abandoning the plan. If so, focus the group on a creative brainstorming session to consider ways of acquiring this resource. (Use Innovative Problem Solving sequence, Activities 59-62, to accomplish this.)

After the brainstorming, see if the group feels it is feasible to proceed with the plan. If so, you probably want to put together a project team to work on this resource area.

If not, discuss the implications of this to the Strategic Plan. Logical questions to explore is:

"Can we still achieve our Purpose, Mission and Vision even if we do not have the resources available now to support some of our action plans?"

"Are there other major goals we could achieve even if we don't have all the resources we require at this time?"

HELP WORKSHEET

In order to carry out your Who Me? Action Plan, what resources will you require? Consider INTERNAL RESOURCES such as: dedication, discipline, a sense of humor, willingness to risk and so forth, as well as EXTERNAL RESOURCES such as: human, technological, financial and so forth. Include in-service training, workshops, conferences and other skill development, educational programs in your EXTERNAL RESOURCES list.

INTERNAL RESOURCES	EXTERNAL RESOURCES
_____	_____
_____	_____
_____	_____
_____	_____
_____	_____
_____	_____
_____	_____
_____	_____
_____	_____
_____	_____
_____	_____
_____	_____
_____	_____
_____	_____
_____	_____
_____	_____
_____	_____
_____	_____

80 Cost/Benefit Analysis

This vision of the future must be formulated in such a way that it will make the pain of changing worth the effort.
—Noel M. Tichy and Mary Anne Devanna

Purpose

Human motivation can be understood in terms of a Cost/Benefit Analysis. Consciously or unconsciously, we weigh the potential payoffs for doing something relative to the possible risks, and if the perceived benefits outweigh the cost, we do it.

The purpose of this activity is for your staff to consider the benefits of the designed changes relative to the costs so that they can tell the truth about the degree to which they are motivated to implement the plan.

Building upon this awareness, the next activity extends the idea by having the group consider how the school's rewards systems could be altered in support of the desired change.

Procedure

1. Hand out copies of the Cost/Benefit Analysis Worksheet.

2. Start with the sample items listed and ask members of your group to put a check next to the suggested costs and benefits they feel are relevant.

3. Next, have the group brainstorm other items to be added to each column.

4. Now, have each person score the relevant items as follows:

Benefits	+ 3	Extremely positive
	+ 2	Moderately positive
	+ 1	Slightly positive
Costs	- 3	Extremely negative
	- 2	Moderately negative
	- 1	Slightly negative

Total each column to determine whether the Benefits outweigh the Costs.

5. Complete the exercise by having each person read his or her scores and discuss the implications in terms of his or her motivation to change.

COST/BENEFIT ANALYSIS WORKSHEET

COSTS		BENEFITS	
____ Students won't get get their needs met	____	____ It is what's best for students	____
____ Test scores may go down	____	____ It is consistent with my values	____
____ Parents will complain	____	____ It will be personally satisfying	____
____ I might not succeed	____	____ It will provide new, exciting challenges	____
____ I'll lose my independence	____	____ It will encourage us to work as a team	____
____ It means more work	____	____ It is an opportunity for me to grow	____
____ I'll lose control	____	____ I will feel more effective	____
____ It is a waste of time	____	____ I will feel more included	____
____ It is a waste of resources	____	____ I will feel more in control	____
____ I will feel uncertain and uncomfortable	____	____ It will provide more financial rewards	____
____ If it doesn't work we'll look like fools	____	____ It will simplify my life	____
____ If it doesn't work, we'll have to start all over again	____	____ It will earn me the approval of others	____

_____   _____

TOTAL -   TOTAL +

81 Rewarding Ideas

If you're going to dangle something in front of them, why limit yourself to carrots?
— From an advertisement for Norwegian Cruise Line

Purpose

In order for change to occur and be sustained, appropriate behaviors need to be reinforced by the organization's system of rewards.

The purpose of this activity is to establish incentives that encourage your staff to act in accord with the desired vision and goals.

Procedure

1. First, as a group, identify the various means of recognizing and rewarding people's performance currently existing in your school or district. Examples include:

    *   salaries (not usually linked to performance, however)
    *   raises (also not usually performance based)
    *   bonuses (mostly nonexistent, unfortunately, in schools)
    *   promotions (also nonexistent)
    *   performance evaluations
    *   recognition from supervisors
    *   recognition from peers
    *   recognition from the community.

2. Next ask each person to identify something that would be an incentive to change. Set this up as a brainstorming session, allowing for unusual and innovative ideas. Record these on easel pages.

    Encourage creativity. Some ideas might be

    *   participation in decision-making
    *   extra field trips
    *   time off for training and development
    *   publishing a book or video documenting the school's change process
    *   cash awards funded by local businesses

- start each staff meeting with acknowledgments of staff members who are making a difference
- highlighting staff contributors in a parent newsletter.

3. Review the "rewarding ideas" generated by the group, and select the ones with the most promise.

4. Put the new ideas together with the first list of existing incentives to create an integrated rewards and recognition program for the school.

5. As a follow-up exercise, repeat the process from the perspective of students.

Epilogue

Perhaps this book takes too limited a view of education being a K-12 process. Maybe the notion of lifelong learning (K-90) is what success in the future will require.

As you use the activities in this book to redesign schools, imagine education being available on any subject, to anyone of any age, anywhere, anytime and anyplace it's needed.

In this vision, do schools as distinct organizations exist? If so, what is their role? What content will students need to know? What process skills will they need to be able to use? What attitudes will they need to possess? What have you learned throughout the course of your life that has made the biggest difference to you?

I would like to think that this book has been of value to you, and that you gained an insight, learned a lesson or acquired a tool that will help you make an even greater contribution to the lives of your students.

For this was my purpose in writing it.

References and Resources

Alexander, Lamar. *America 2000: An Education Strategy.* Washington, D.C.: U.S. Department of Education, 1991.

Barth, Roland S. *Improving Schools from Within: Teachers, Parents and Principals Can Make the Difference.* San Francisco: Jossey-Bass, 1990.

Bullard, Pamela and Barbara O. Taylor. *Making School Reform Happen.* Boston: Allyn and Bacon, 1993.

Burns, James Mac Gregor. *Leadership.* New York: Harper & Row, 1978.

Canfield, Jack and Frank Siccone. *101 Ways to Develop Student Self-Esteem and Responsibility.* Boston: Allyn and Bacon, 1993.

Cunningham, William C. and Donn W. Gresso. *Cultural Leadership: The Culture of Excellence in Education.* Boston: Allyn and Bacon, 1993

Covey, Stephen R. *The 7 Habits of Highly Effective People.* New York: Simon and Schuster, 1989.

Davis, Brian L. et al. editors. *Successful Managers Handbook.* Minneapolis: Personnel Decisions, 1989.

Doyle, Michael and David Straus. *How to Make Meetings Work.* New York: Jove, 1976.

Finn, Chester E. Jr. *We Must Take Charge: Our Schools and Our Future.* New York: Free Press, 1991.

Fiske, Edward B. *Smart Schools, Smart Kids: Why Do Some Schools Work?* New York: Touchstone, 1992.

Fournies, Ferdinand F. *Coaching for Improved Work Performance.* Blue Ridge Summit, PA: Liberty Hall Press, 1987.

Gazda, George M. et al. *Human Relations Development: A Manual for Educators.* Boston: Allyn and Bacon, 1984.

Goens, George A. and Sharon I. R. Clover. *Mastering School Reform.* Boston: Allyn and Bacon, 1991.

Hersey, Paul and Kenneth Blanchard. *Situational Leadership.* New York: Warner, 1985.

Kinlaw, Dennis C. *Coaching for Commitment: Managerial Strategies for Obtaining Superior Performance.* San Diego: University Associates, 1989.

Lakein, Alan. *How to Get Control of Your Time and Your Life.* New York: New American Library, 1973.

Mackenzie, Alec. *The Time Trap.* New York: American Management Association, 1990.

National Commission of Excellence in Education. *A Nation at Risk: The Imperative for School Reform.* Washington, D.C.: U.S. Office of Education, 1983.

Parker, Glenn M. *Team Players and Teamwork: The New Competitive Business Strategy.* San Francisco: Jossey-Bass, 1990.

Peters, Tom and Nancy Austin. *A Passion for Excellence.* New York: Random House, 1985.

Von Oech, Roger. *A Kick in the Seat of the Pants.* New York: Harper & Row, 1986.

Whitaker, Kathryn S. and Monte C. Moses, *The Restructuring Handbook: A Guide to School Revitalization.* Boston: Allyn and Bacon, 1994.

Wilson, Stephanie. *The Organized Executive.* New York: Warner, 1983.

SICCONE INSTITUTE offers workshops and training programs for schools and businesses in areas such as: Facilitative Leadership, Manager as Coach, Restructuring and Strategic Planning, Communication and Teamwork, Teacher Empowerment, and Student Self-Esteem and Responsibility.

For further information contact:

SICCONE INSTITUTE
2151 Union Street
San Francisco, CA 94123
415/922-2244